RAMEN
OBSESSION

THE ULTIMATE BIBLE FOR MASTERING JAPANESE RAMEN

NAOMI IMATOME-YUN AND ROBIN DONOVAN

PHOTOGRAPHY BY ANTONIS ACHILLEOS

ROCKRIDGE
PRESS

For general information on our other products and services or to obtain technical support, please contact our Customer Care Department within the United States at (866) 744-2665, or outside the United States at (510) 253-0500.

Rockridge Press publishes its books in a variety of electronic and print formats. Some content that appears in print may not be available in electronic books, and vice versa.

Cover recipe: Shoyu Wild Mushroom Ramen with Meyer Lemon and Kabocha Squash, page 110
Interior and Cover Designer: Diana Haas
Photo Art Director: Janice Ackerman
Editor: Jesse Aylen
Food styling by Rishon Hanners; Prop styling by Mindi Shapiro
Map Illustration: Merideth Harte
Production Editor: Ashley Polikoff

ISBN: Print 978-1-64152-584-8 | eBook 978-1-64152-585-5
RO

For our loves Doug, Cashel, Lucas, and Zeke.

And to all the travelers, mavericks,
and noodle lovers.

CONTENTS

INTRODUCTION

RAMEN-OBSESSED

I grew up loving ramen, specifically that red and white Sapporo Ichiban instant noodle package. It was a different era, when third graders could boil water, and I loved making myself an after-school "home-cooked meal" of Ichiban, a swirled egg, and a scoop of rice.

Although I slurped ramen at Asian food stalls, I didn't fall in love with true restaurant ramen until visiting New York's Momofuku Noodle Bar when it first opened. Since I was a restaurant reviewer, I was overeating regularly, but I was shocked by how heartwarming my Momofuku experience was; though I'd eaten ramen across three continents, I was instantly transported.

Creating that balanced bowl at home seems daunting, but it's surprisingly doable. Start with the most basic components, and master them before moving on to create the bowl of your dreams. Even the simplest pairing of noodles and broth can be intensely beautiful, and as my conversations with some of the world's best ramen chefs have revealed, it's an expansive, global, and democratic dish.

WHAT'S INSIDE THIS BOOK AND HOW TO USE IT

Ramen at its simplest is easy to understand: noodles and broth, which usually come with a range of distinct toppings. Often, it's seasoned with aromatic oil and a seasoning sauce called *tare* that the cook drizzles in the bottom of the bowl before ladling in the broth. However, it requires the right balance to get all the components singing together.

With care and precision, we break down the essential steps to making the five ramen components: the broth, the tare, the aromatic oils, the noodles, and the toppings. With this ramen-making tool kit, you can master the craft and assemble delicious bowls in your own kitchen.

This book is divided into three parts. In part 1, we introduce you to ramen's storied and layered past. Part 2 takes you through each individual component in a step-by-step format. Finally, part 3 serves up the recipes so that you can create your own vivid and delicious bowls at home.

Consider this book a primer and encyclopedia for the ramen-obsessed.

THE RECIPES

While most cookbooks aren't meant to be read from cover to cover, if you're new to the craft of ramen, reading through many of these recipes will give you a good foundation and help you develop your ramen sense. Together, we'll explore the breadth of possibilities contained in such a simple-seeming bowl. From Spicy Miso Ramen with Chicken Karaage and Swiss Chard (page 148) to Hakata-Style Mountain of Scallions Ramen (page 83) to delicious vegan and vegetarian varieties, this is a master class in the wide world of ramen.

Ramen is intensely regional, and the dish changes depending on the climate, season, and prefecture (county) of its surroundings. As it's made its way around the world, it's evolved even further.

We've included easy and more challenging recipes suited for home use, and even with the intense ramen focus, you'll learn to create other dishes, from toppings like succulent pork to flavor-bombs like Japanese pickles and gyoza.

Ramen can seem like such an insurmountable feat, yet almost all of the work is done in advance. Once you've created the broths and noodles, tare and toppings, it takes only minutes to assemble your meal.

Although I created some of the recipes in this book myself, the vast majority were crafted by Robin Donovan, a talented recipe developer with the hyper-focus and culinary knowledge needed for a ramen bible.

PART I

THE RAMEN STORY: WELCOMED CREATIVITY IN A WORLD STEEPED WITH TRADITION

Ramen enjoys a special place in the hearts of Japanese people, and a unique position in Japanese cuisine for how quickly it became popular and how much it has evolved over time. By increasing your knowledge of this beloved noodle dish and understanding its history and culture, you'll appreciate the ramen you make at home even more.

THE HISTORY OF RAMEN

The most widely accepted history of ramen is that it journeyed to Japan from China, although since noodles-in-broth was already a part of Japanese cuisine, the concept was not wholly novel. The well-known springy noodles in chicken broth, however, found their way into Japan in the 19th century through Chinese merchants, and in a country where the culinary culture is steeped in tradition, beauty, and reverence, ramen is a relative newcomer.

JAPANESE CUISINE AND TRADITIONS

Japanese *itamae* (head chefs) receive years of apprenticeship and education, learning from a master itamae and then working as a sous chef before they can reach the itamae role. In Japan, being a chef is often a family business, with third- or fourth-generation chefs running their family restaurants.

But some of the country's best and most-loved *ramen-ya* (ramen shops) are total newcomers. Because ramen's popularity is relatively new and there are no rules set in stone, even completely unknown chefs have made their mark on ramen culture.

CHINESE INFLUENCE

Ramen's history in Japan is a tale of imperialism, migration, and occupation. In 1853, Japan reluctantly opened its ports to American trade, a shift that opened the door to trade agreements with other countries, and exposed Japan to outside influence following centuries of closed borders.

Yokohama was the first port opened to foreign trade, in 1859, and maintains a large Chinatown today. Chinese travelers and migrants brought a dish of noodles in a chicken broth called *Nanking soba* (named after the capital of China) to Japan and started serving it from food carts. By 1910, the first specialized ramen-ya started serving the dish, which came to be known as *Shina soba* (Chinese noodles). However, it remained mostly a stall and cart food popular with blue-collar and foreign workers.

During 1945, the last year of World War II, Japan suffered one of the worst rice harvests in decades, and the American occupiers flooded the Japanese market with cheap flour and lard. In three years, Japan tripled their bread consumption and ramen exploded in popularity as a cheap and filling meal.

During the post war period, Shina soba became known as *Chuka soba* (using another word for "Chinese"), after "Shina" was deemed a derogatory imperial term for Chinese people.

BIRTH OF JAPANESE FAST FOOD

In 1958, Momofuku Ando invented packaged instant noodles and called them ramen. (Yes, New York's famous Momofuku restaurant pays homage to instant ramen's founder!) The "ra" comes from the Chinese word for "pulled" (*la*, pronounced with a sound between an "L" and an "R" that we don't have in English) and the "men" comes from the word for "noodles" (*mien*). Shortly after 1958, the Japanese economy took off and more small shops began selling ramen. Subsequent decades witnessed ramen-ya opening across the country and a growing love of packaged ramen, but it wasn't until the 1990s that the real ramen boom began in Japan.

Ramen was, for most of its history in Japan, inexpensive fast food, and even today, most ramen restaurants have few seats and very limited menus. Until close to the turn of the 21st century, most ramen shops in Japan were still the equivalent of local hole-in-the-wall joints in the States: cheap, quick, and filling.

RAMEN CULTURE

Ramen is still "fast food" in the sense that it's meant to be eaten quickly while piping hot, but it no longer carries a low-quality connotation. It's now a national icon, though still inexpensive. You can get a great bowl for under $10 all over the country.

Deep love exists for ramen in Japan, with more than 6,000 ramen shops in Tokyo alone and more than 10,000 in the country. There are ramen-themed magazines, books, museums, tours, TV shows, and countless websites. In 2015, Tsuta was the first ramen-ya to earn a Michelin star. In keeping with authenticity, the restaurant seats only nine people.

Hiroshi Shimakage, a cofounder of the Ramen Beast app, says, "The history of ramen is still short, but always changing. Especially after 1996, when so many kinds of ramen shops opened. Now the ramen scene is changing more quickly. There is a new kind of trend every year. Many ramen masters want to try or create new styles, and new shops open almost every week."

Ohsaki-san, Japan's preeminent ramen critic, also cites 1996 as a turning point: "The Internet started. Customers began putting images of ramen on the Internet. Before that, a ramen maker could visit different ramen shops and just steal their techniques. After 1996, you could see if one ramen shop was a copy of another. Ramen shops had to start developing original styles."

AN EVERYDAY STAPLE

The typical ramen-ya is intensely focused. This attention to detail is the foundation of Japanese craft: By turning your attention to one thing, you master it. Despite the craftsmanship that goes into each bowl, ramen culture doesn't inspire lingering; most ramen-yas are still small counter shops. Many urban ramen-ya are also partly automated. You select your items from a visual menu, pay for your order, and hand your ticket to the cashier or put it on the counter when you sit down. Then your ramen arrives.

Ramen is meant to be eaten fast since it tastes best piping hot, so ramen restaurants often encourage solo dining. Ichiran, a Japanese restaurant chain that's expanded to New York, goes so far as to include actual wooden partitions between the individual seats.

NO RULES

Even though ramen has been in Japan since the 19th century, it didn't capture the cultural imagination until recently. In fact, part of its global appeal is that it's new and unencumbered by years of tradition. Ivan Orkin, a classically trained chef who holds the distinction as the only American to succeed in Japan's ramen scene, describes ramen as a cuisine with few rules. "[Ramen is] unlike sushi, tempura, *washoku*, *kaiseki*, French, Italian— for which there are reams written about the different techniques and how you should do it."

Japanese food expert and *Iron Chef America* judge Akiko Katayama agrees that part of the appeal of ramen is its flexibility, saying, "Ramen is a unique comfort food that allows a lot of creativity, like pasta. Ramen is establishing its own path in the U.S., and I think it will stay with us for a long time."

REGIONAL RAMEN

In Japan, seasonal cooking can refer to 72 microseasons, featuring the best local food of each week, or even every few days. Similarly, Japanese cuisine has always featured regional variations based on the best local food. Inland cities use mountain herbs and vegetables, and coastal cities feature the best seafood and vegetables. Because local cooking has always been part of Japanese culture, we'll look at some of the most renowned variations of this versatile bowl.

HOKKAIDO

Hokkaido is the most northern of the four main islands of Japan, with cold winters, heavy snow, subzero temperatures, and milder summers. As the most sparsely populated island, it's a popular destination for nature lovers, skiers, snowboarders, and campers.

The three major cities of Hokkaido (Sapporo, Hakodate, and Asahikawa) each have their own distinct and celebrated ramen styles. The Hokkaido airport, New Chitose Airport, even has a Ramen Dojo, a special section in the terminal with 10 different ramen shops showcasing their local styles.

Sapporo

Sapporo is the birthplace of miso ramen, which has been served since the 1960s and features a broth that's *tonkotsu* stock (pork bone marrow) or a blend of tonkotsu and chicken stock. Flavored with a miso tare, it's richly seasoned and often covered with a fine layer of oil that prevents the heat from escaping during Sapporo's harsh winters. Sapporo ramen uses thick, yellow noodles and often includes toppings such as *chashu* (sliced roasted pork), *menma* (seasoned bamboo shoots), sliced scallions, sweet corn, other vegetables, or butter.

Hakodate

As a port city, Hakodate's ramen arrived in the late 1800s from Chinese merchants. Kelp and seafood show up in the city's bowls. Often, the ramen features a light, clear broth with thin, straight noodles. Most of Hakodate's ramen-yas are *shio* ramens (seasoned with salty tare), and use either a tonkotsu or chicken stock base, or a chicken broth and kelp (or other seafood) base. Hakodate's ramen doesn't feature the high fat content of its neighboring cities, and the basic toppings are chashu, menma, scallions, bean sprouts, and soft-boiled eggs. Seafood ramen bowls here may also include kelp or other seafood, like crab or ebi shrimp.

Asahikawa
The northernmost city of Hokkaido's three big ramen cities, Asahikawa is located in the island's center. The ramen complements winter with a thin layer of flavored oil on top of the broth that traps the bowl's heat. Asahikawa ramen is a *shoyu* ramen with a "double broth"—a blend of tonkotsu and fish-based broths seasoned with a soy sauce tare and thick, wavy noodles to soak up the flavor and oil. Although Asahikawa is a noncoastal city, it was a hub to transport seafood throughout the island, so you can find seafood in abundance. The ramen in the region, also known for its pork farms, further reflects the best of the local ingredients.

FUKUSHIMA

One of Japan's least densely populated prefectures, Fukushima is about 160 miles north of Tokyo and known for its natural beauty, its *onsens* (hot springs), seasonal fruits such as white peaches, and Kitakata ramen. Kitakata is the famous ramen city in Fukushima, and along with Sapporo and Hakata, one of the three major regional ramen styles in the country.

Kitakata
A small city of roughly 50,000 people in western Fukushima, Kitakata is a mountain-ringed town with more than 120 ramen shops. It's a picturesque destination with rice fields and charming old storehouses (*kura*) that have been converted into inns and shops. Kitakata's first ramen-ya opened in 1926, and people here love the dish so much that a local custom (called *asa-ra*) is to enjoy ramen for breakfast.

Kitakata ramen has a delicate, clear broth usually made with pork bones, chicken bones, and *niboshi* (dried anchovies or sardines). It's flavored with the locally produced soy sauce that is kept in the storehouses around town, and usually topped with chashu, *naruto* (a pink-and-white fish cake), menma, and scallions. Kitakata ramen is most distinctive for its thick, flat, and curly noodles (called *takasuimen*), which are slipperier and softer than other noodles.

FUKUOKA

This prefecture on the southern island of Kyushu is surrounded by the ocean on three sides and features a subtropical climate. For nearly 100 years, the region's mobile food stalls (*yatai*) have been serving ramen, and Hakata ramen is Fukuoka's most famous food. When people refer to Fukuoka, Kyushu, or Hakata ramen, they are generally referring to the region's milky, thick tonkotsu broth ramen. Ippudo, a popular ramen chain with outlets in New York City and Sydney, is a Fukuoka brand.

Hakata

A bustling seaside city in Fukuoka, Hakata is home to some of the most famous ramen in Japan. Made from long-simmering pork bones until it becomes thick, rich, and gelatinous broth, the dish includes thin, straight, al dente Hakata ramen noodles. One of the most well-known styles in the West, the stick-to-your-ribs soup is addictively satisfying. Hakata is also home to the *kaedama* system, in which you can order a second or third serving of noodles to eat with the creamy broth.

TOKYO

In Tokyo, the nation's capital, and an international city, you can find almost every type of Japanese ramen style. However, for many Japanese people, the Tokyo shoyu ramen has always been the quintessential definition of a bowl of ramen. Tokyo-style ramen is distinctive because the broth is made partly with *dashi* (Japanese seafood stock). Many food stalls originally made and served noodle soups in dashi, and the practice continued in the making of Tokyo ramen.

Tokyo

Although Tokyo is home to countless ramen styles, the original capital ramen is topped with bean sprouts, chewy and wavy noodles, chopped scallions, slow-cooked soft-boiled egg (*nitamago*), chashu, and kamaboko. The shoyu broth is brown, made of both dashi and chicken bones and flavored by a soy sauce tare.

Tsukemen

A newer invention from the 1950s by ramen maker Yamagishi Kazuo, tsuke-men is a type of ramen in which the noodles and soup are served separately, letting a diner dip the noodles into the broth mixture, which is thick and bursting with flavor. Tsukemen noodles are served cold, ensuring they stay firm, plump, and chewy. Depending upon the weather, the soup or sauce can be hot or cold, and goes perfectly with kaedama (an extra serving of noodles). Popular toppings include seaweed, soft-boiled eggs, chashu, and vegetables.

WAKAYAMA

The Wakayama prefecture, located south of Osaka in the Kansai region, is a mix of wild landscapes, mountains, temples, and shrines. As the center of Shingon Buddhism, it has a long history of pilgrim travelers making their way across its trails. The ramen boom here is relatively new, and thanks to a 1998 poll by a popular TV show that deemed a tiny shop, Ide Shoten, the country's best, ramen lovers make pilgrimages here.

Chuka Soba

Locals call ramen "Chuka soba" (Chinese noodles) here, and Ide Shoten is still considered one of the best ramen shops in Japan. They serve between 600 and 1,000 bowls every day, with their specialty a tonkotsu-shoyu broth with thin, straight noodles. The other Wakayama ramen style has a lighter shoyu broth, but both are topped in a simple fashion, with chashu, menma, bean sprouts, and scallions.

A custom in Wakayama is eating salted mackerel sushi (*hayazushi*) with a bowl of ramen. Diners help themselves to the table's boiled eggs and mackerel and, upon leaving, tell the cashier how much they ate. Given this regional practice, Wakayama's ramen bowls are not overly large.

KYOTO

Kyoto, Japan's former capital and one of its most beautiful cities, boasts picturesque shrines, palaces, hot springs, and beaches. Visitors flock there for the cherry blossoms, autumn foliage, and Kyoto's famous food culture. Kyoto's local ramen has a bold, rich, and thick flavor and consistency, featuring straight noodles. Chicken shoyu ramen is popular, as are broths made from a combination of chicken, pork bones, and seafood broth (dashi). Kyoto's ramen (even when made with chicken broth) has a thicker consistency and mouthfeel, with a rich umami flavor. Common toppings are chashu, chopped scallions, menma, nori, and a pat of butter.

Takayama

Located at the base of the Japanese Alps, Takayama is famous for its sushi (which features fresh seafood from nearby Toyama), its Hida (a type of wagyu beef), and its ramen. Takayama broth is usually made from chicken bones, bonito stock, and soy sauce. Unlike most Japanese ramen-ya which use tare to flavor the broth, Takayama ramen shops boil the seasoning ingredients together with the broth, then top it with thin, curly noodles. As they do in Wakayama, the Takayama residents often call ramen Chuka soba.

HIROSHIMA

Although this coastal prefecture is perhaps best-known for its atomic bombing, Hiroshima's city has been rebuilt into a thriving metropolis recognized for its peace advocacy. Famous for its regional cuisine, including oysters, squid, octopus, and a savory Japanese pancake (called *okonomiyaki*), the city also hosts a few different styles of ramen: Hiroshima tsukemen, *tantanmen,* and Hiroshima ramen.

Tantanmen is a popular, Japanese-adapted version of Chinese dan dan noodles, a regional favorite. However, Hiroshima's version lacks broth, and the noodles arrive separately from the spicy sauce. To enjoy, the diner swirls the noodles in the sauce to fully coat them (30 times is the recommended number!), and uses such table spices as chili peppers, Japanese *sansho,* and vinegar to season before eating. The sansho (Sichuan peppercorn) is the spice of choice and adds a delightfully fizzy numbing sensation.

As elsewhere in Japan, Hiroshima tsukemen features cold dipping noodles, but its sauce is hot and spicy with chili oil and peppers, and often the bowl is topped with cabbage, scallions, soft-boiled eggs, and chashu.

Onomichi

Onomichi is known for its beautiful, temple-covered sloping hills and calm seaport city—and, more recently, for its adorable cat population. Onomichi's ramen has a clear broth made from local small fish sourced from the Seto Inland Sea. Served piping hot with a top layer of hot oil, the local ramen also features small chunks of pork fat (*seabura*).

REGIONAL MAP OF JAPANESE RAMEN

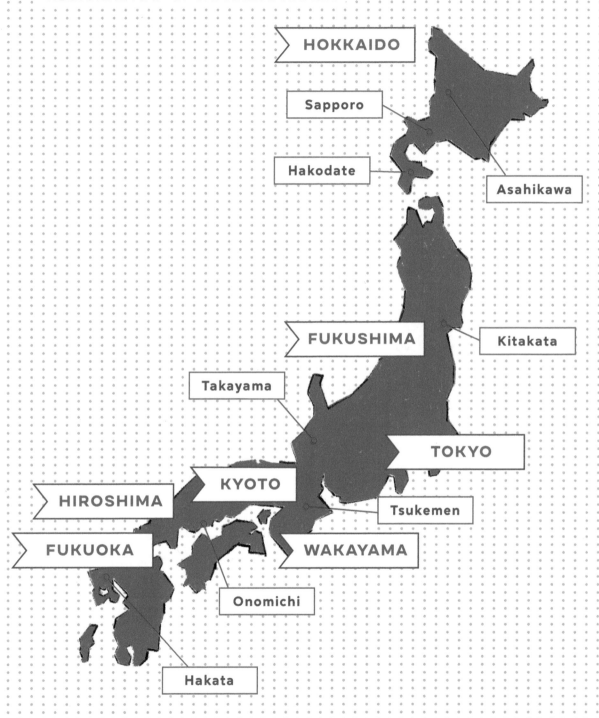

HOKKAIDO

Sapporo

Hakodate

Asahikawa

FUKUSHIMA

Kitakata

Takayama

TOKYO

KYOTO

HIROSHIMA

Tsukemen

FUKUOKA

WAKAYAMA

Onomichi

Hakata

RAMEN OBSESSION AROUND THE WORLD

Although today's ramen has its roots in a Chinese soup, it's become its own distinctly Japanese dish. In Japan, as we've seen, ramen is a regional dish adapted to different climates, ingredients, and tastes, so it should only make sense that it has been adopted—and adapted—by countries around the world, incorporating truly global influences.

NOT MEANT TO BE AUTHENTIC

Ivan Orkin, probably the only American chef to succeed in Japan's ramen world, rose to fame in Tokyo with his refined double-soup ramen (chicken and dashi broths). He owns two shops in New York City and two in Tokyo, but first impressed Japan's top ramen critic, Ohsaki-san, with his addition of slow-roasted tomatoes as a topping.

One popular Colorado ramen shop has a bowl with confit duck, arugula, and apples; one of Hawaii's chains has a creation of black garlic oil, garlic butter, and Parmesan cheese; and some Florida ramens feature combinations of local corn and Gulf shrimp. Chef Gregg Des Rosier, owner of Wisconsin's Tochi Ramen, says that Japanese patrons at his restaurant often order his Milwaukee-style ramen with seared flank steak and smoked bone marrow butter. Like many others, it fulfills two important elements: It's distinctly regional and uses local ingredients.

WORLD LANDSCAPE OF RAMEN

Outside Japan, the ramen boom started in New York City, with Momofuku Noodle Bar in 2004, and this satisfying bowl has been making its way around the world ever since. Some shops in London include cock scratchings (fried chicken skins) as a topping, Milan's earliest ramen-ya has a swirl of olive oil and pepperoncini on top, and duck makes an appearance on South Africa's ramen-ya menus. The endless ingredient combinations represent how this dish can morph to take on the flavor of its creators and the local delicacies. Keep this in mind as you embark on the adventure of creating your own ramen bowls.

PART II

THE SIX STEPS

Even though it can take just a few minutes for your ramen cook to whip up the bowl in front of you—a dash of sauce, a pour of broth, a ladleful of fresh noodles, and a waterfall of toppings—the flavors in the final slurp-worthy meal are the result of careful planning. These mother recipes cover ramen's essential elements: broth, tare (seasoning sauce), noodles, aromatic oils and fats, and the all-important toppings. With these foundational recipes, you'll have a tool kit to create countless ramen varieties.

STEP 1: SOUP/BROTH

- **Clear Chicken Broth (*Tori Chintan*)**
- **"Creamy" Chicken Broth (*Tori Paitan*)**
- **Tonkotsu (Pork Bone Broth)**
- **Pork and Chicken Broth**
- **Awase Dashi**
- **Shiitake Dashi**

The ramen broth provides the body of the dish, but unlike most Western broths, it can contain just a couple of ingredients, often just pork or chicken parts. Since most of the flavoring in the soup comes from the tare, the seasoning sauce spooned into the bottom of the bowl, the broth itself isn't heavily seasoned. There are also "double broth" ramens, which combine two different broths—for example, a pork bone broth and a more traditional dashi made from bonito flakes and kombu seaweed in the same bowl.

Ramen is unique because there are many different ways to categorize the dozens of different styles. People often mistakenly refer to ramen broth as "shio broth" or "miso broth," even though the terms "shio" and "miso" refer to the tare that flavor the broth. A shio tare can season a chicken broth or a milky pork bone broth (tonkotsu). The correct way to distinguish ramen broth is by the ingredients used to make it, not the sauce used to flavor it. However, you *can* distinguish your finished bowl of ramen by referring to the seasoning sauce and the broth, or just one or the other. For example, miso tonkotsu refers to the tare and the broth, but Tokyo miso ramen refers to just the tare seasoning sauce, not the chicken stock with which it is traditionally made.

A broth's heaviness is another classification: *Kotteri* broths are thicker and often opaque, the product of simmering bones for a long time, while *assari* broths are thinner and usually clear, the end product of fish, vegetables, or bones cooked for a shorter length of time. Some people also use the terms *paitan* (white soup) and *chintan* (clear soup).

SHOPPING LIST

Here are the main ingredients you'll need to make your ramen broths:

- **Bonito flakes (Bonito is a type of tuna, and bonito flakes [*katsuobushi*] are made from tuna that's been dried and smoked. The flakes are shaved pieces of this dried and smoked fish.)**
- **Carrots**
- **Chicken bones (You can use chicken legs, backs or frames, necks, wings, and so forth. You can also buy a whole chicken and remove the meat before cooking the bones, or boil it whole and use the cooked meat as a topping.)**
- **Chicken feet**
- **Chicken wings**
- **Dried shiitake mushrooms (Shiitake and porcini mushrooms**
make a deep, rich stock for vegetable ramen.)
- **Garlic**
- **Ginger**
- **Kombu (Sometimes seen as "konbu," this dried seaweed is a good source of glutamic acid, which is responsible for umami flavor. To make dashi, you should buy the thick and wide sheets of kombu.)**
- **Onions**
- **Pigs' feet**
- **Pork belly**
- **Pork bones (You can use legs, backs or frames, necks, and so forth.)**
- **Scallions**

EQUIPMENT LIST

Here are your must-have kitchen tools for cooking broths:

- **Fine-mesh sieve**
- **Large colander**
- **Large slotted spoon**
- **Large stockpot**
- **Long-handled wooden spoon**
- **Saucepan**
- **Sharp knife**
- **Soup ladle**
- **Storage containers (Glass bottles or large jars with a tight seal work best.)**

These optional appliances are nice to have:

- **Electric pressure cooker (An Instant Pot or something similar is excellent.)**
- **Slow cooker**

PREPPING AND COOKING

Preparation is the key to making a killer bowl of ramen since the actual assembly of the ingredients takes mere minutes. Although some people might want to dedicate an entire day to making ramen, it's easiest to make a lot of the ingredients in advance. Your broth will keep for days in the refrigerator and weeks in the freezer, as do the tare and many of the toppings. In addition, you can use your broth, tare, and toppings to form the foundations of countless other dishes.

For cooking chicken and pork broths, one essential step you should not skip is the rinsing and parboiling of the bones. Although it's not something we usually do in American cooking, it is essential for getting a clearer and cleaner-tasting broth. In preparation, rinse your bones well in running water, and then boil them for at least 20 minutes before making your broth. Since the long-simmering that follows will extract the flavor and body from the bones and the marrow, don't worry that you are throwing the best part down the drain.

CLEAR CHICKEN BROTH (*TORI CHINTAN*)

DAIRY-FREE, GLUTEN-FREE, NUT-FREE, SOY-FREE

PREP TIME: 10 minutes, plus 4 hours to chill / **COOK TIME:** stovetop, 6 hours; pressure cooker, 90 minutes

MAKES ABOUT 2 QUARTS

Unlike Western broths, Japanese ramen broth isn't fortified with aromatics, vegetables, and herbs: Simplicity is the name of the game. The broth's seasoning and flavor come from the tare, infused fats and oils, noodles, and a galaxy of toppings. The broth itself should taste of the type of bones from which it is made. It doesn't need to be completely clear and the tasty and nutritious bits shouldn't be meticulously strained out since they add to the flavor and texture. The collagen in the chicken feet gives this hearty broth its rich flavor and lush mouthfeel. Although it's possible to make a good broth without the feet (just add more bones), expect a thinner and lighter result.

1 pound chicken feet

1 pound chicken wings

3 pounds chicken bones

10 to 12 cups water

PREPARATION

Blanch the chicken feet. Place them in a stockpot and cover with 2 to 3 inches of tap water. Set the pot over high heat and bring to a boil. When the water boils, immediately remove the pot from the heat and strain, discarding the water.

STOVETOP METHOD

1. Place the chicken wings and bones in the bottom of the (cleaned) stockpot and then place the chicken feet on top. Cover the bones and feet with the water (the bones should be covered by at least 2 inches of water).

2. Set the pot over low heat and bring to a simmer. Cover and continue to simmer, without stirring, for about 6 hours.

3. Using a colander, strain the broth. Cover and chill in the refrigerator for at least 4 hours.

4. When the broth is fully chilled, skim the fat off the top and save it to season your ramen (page 34).

Continued

PRESSURE COOKER METHOD

1. Place the chicken wings and bones in the bottom of the pressure cooker and top with the chicken feet. Cover the bones and feet with the water (the bones should be covered by at least 2 inches of water). Cover the pot, seal the valve, and cook on high pressure for 90 minutes. Let the pressure release naturally.

2. Using a colander, strain the broth. Cover and chill in the refrigerator for at least 4 hours.

3. When the broth is fully chilled, skim the fat off the top and save it to season your ramen (page 34).

Storage Tip: *Regardless of cooking method, you can store the broth, covered, in the refrigerator for up to 1 week or in the freezer for up to 3 months.*

Repurposing Tip: *Save the bones once you've strained them out of your broth and use them to make* **Tori Paitan**, *a thick, creamy, white chicken broth (page 19).*

"CREAMY" CHICKEN BROTH (*TORI PAITAN*)

DAIRY-FREE, GLUTEN-FREE, NUT-FREE, SOY-FREE

PREP TIME: 10 minutes, plus 4 hours to chill / **COOK TIME:** stovetop, 9 hours; pressure cooker, 4 hours

MAKES ABOUT 2 QUARTS

Tori paitan is a creamy, thick chicken broth made by boiling bones to encourage them to give up their collagen and marrow. You can make Tori Paitan starting with fresh bones, or you can reuse the bones that you've already used to make Tori Chintan (page 17). If doing the latter, skip the blanching step.

1 pound chicken feet

1 pound chicken wings

3 pounds chicken bones

10 to 12 cups water

½ carrot, sliced

½ onion, sliced

5 or 6 scallions, white parts only (roots removed)

1- or 2-inch piece of ginger, sliced

10 garlic cloves, peeled

PREPARATION

Blanch the chicken feet, wings, and bones. Place them in a stockpot and cover with 2 to 3 inches of tap water. Set the pot over high heat and bring to a boil. When the water boils, immediately remove the pot from the heat and strain, discarding the water.

STOVETOP METHOD

1. Place the chicken wings and bones in the bottom of the (cleaned) stockpot and then place the chicken feet on top. Cover the bones and feet with the water (the bones should be covered by at least 2 inches of water).

2. Set the pot over medium-high heat and bring to a boil. Reduce the heat to medium, cover, and boil for 6 to 8 hours, until the broth is creamy white and the bones have broken down.

3. Add the carrot, onion, scallions, ginger, and garlic and boil for 1 hour more.

4. Using a colander, strain the broth. Cover and chill in the refrigerator for at least 4 hours.

5. When the broth is fully chilled, skim the fat off the top and save it to season your ramen (page 34).

Continued

PRESSURE COOKER METHOD

1. Place the chicken wings and bones in the bottom of the pressure cooker and place the chicken feet on top. Cover the bones and feet with the water (the bones should be covered by at least 2 inches of water). Cover the pot, seal the valve, and cook on high pressure for 2 hours. Quick release the pressure.

2. Either in the pressure cooker (if using an electric pressure cooker with a sauté function) or in a stockpot on the stovetop over medium-high heat, bring the stock back up to a rapid boil. Continue to boil until the stock is creamy white and the bones have broken down, about 1 hour.

3. Add the carrot, onion, scallions, ginger, and garlic and boil for 1 hour more.

4. Using a colander, strain the broth. Cover and chill in the refrigerator for at least 4 hours.

5. When the broth is fully chilled, skim the fat off the top and save it to season your ramen (page 34).

Storage Tip: *Regardless of cooking method, you can store the broth, covered, in the refrigerator for up to 1 week or in the freezer for up to 3 months.*

TONKOTSU (PORK BONE BROTH)

DAIRY-FREE, GLUTEN-FREE, NUT-FREE, SOY-FREE

PREP TIME: 10 minutes, plus 3 hours to chill / **COOK TIME:** stovetop, 10 hours; pressure cooker, 4 hours

MAKES ABOUT 3 QUARTS

Tonkotsu is often called the king of ramen broths because it is one of the most common, sumptuously flavored broths. Made from pork bones, water, and an onion, a good tonkotsu is milky and opaque, with a rich, concentrated flavor from the fat, collagen, and cartilage that melts into the broth.

3 pounds pork bones, cut into 2-inch pieces

2 pounds pigs' feet, halved

1 onion, peeled and halved

12 to 16 cups filtered water

PREPARATION

1. Blanch the pork bones and pigs' feet. Place them in a large stockpot, cover with cold tap water, and set over high heat. As soon as the water comes to a full boil, remove the pot from the heat. Drain the pot, discarding the water. Rinse the bones well under cold water.

2. Refrigerate the blanched, rinsed bones and feet for about 3 hours.

STOVETOP METHOD

1. Place the bones, feet, and the onion in a clean stockpot and cover them with the water (the bones and onion should be covered by at least 2 inches of water). Set over high heat and bring to a rolling boil. Reduce the heat to medium. Skim off and discard any brown foam that rises to the top. Boil for 8 hours. The liquid will reduce as the stock cooks. During the boiling process, add water as needed to keep the bones covered.

2. After 8 hours, raise the heat to high and bring the water to a boil again. With a wooden spoon, move the bones around to encourage them to release their marrow. Continue to boil until there is no cartilage or soft tissue left on the bones and they are almost bare, 1 to 2 hours more.

3. Strain the stock into a clean stockpot or large bowl. Discard the solids. Let the stock cool to room temperature, then cover and refrigerate for at least 4 hours. The stock will be milky white and gelatinous.

Continued

4. When the broth is fully chilled, skim the fat off the top and reserve it to season your ramen (page 34).

PRESSURE COOKER METHOD

1. Place the blanched, rinsed, and chilled bones and the onion in a stovetop or electric pressure cooker and add the water (the bones should be covered by at least 2 inches of water). Lock the top, seal the valve, and cook on high pressure for 2 hours. Quick release the pressure and then let the stock sit for at least 1 hour.

2. Bring the stock back to a boil, either in the pressure cooker (uncovered) or by transferring it to a clean stockpot. Continue to boil until there is no cartilage or soft tissue left on the bones and they look bare, adding water as needed to keep the water level high, 1 to 2 hours more.

3. Strain the stock into a clean stockpot or large bowl. Discard the solids. Let the stock cool to room temperature, then cover and refrigerate for at least 4 hours. The stock will be milky white and gelatinous.

4. When the broth is fully chilled, skim the fat off the top and reserve it to season your ramen (page 34).

Storage Tip: *Regardless of cooking method, you can store the broth, covered, in the refrigerator for up to 1 week or in the freezer for up to 3 months.*

Ingredient Tip: *Use the best-quality pork bones you can find, ideally organic. The feet provide collagen, so don't omit them (if you are unable to locate them, substitute additional shank bones, cut into 2-inch pieces). Ask your butcher to halve them for you.*

PORK AND CHICKEN BROTH

DAIRY-FREE, GLUTEN-FREE, NUT-FREE, SOY-FREE

PREP TIME: 10 minutes, plus 4 hours to chill / **COOK TIME:** stovetop, 4 hours; pressure cooker, 1 hour

MAKES ABOUT 3 QUARTS

Ramen broth made with chicken *or* pork bones are the most common, but it isn't unusual to find broth made with both, and this broth benefits from the rich flavors of both types of bones. It's thick with collagen from the pork bones, but less so than a Tonkotsu.

1 chicken carcass

1 pound pork bones, cut into
   2-inch pieces

1 (4-inch) square
   piece of kombu

½ pound pork belly

4 dried shiitake mushrooms

1 (3-inch) piece fresh ginger,
   peeled and sliced into thick
   rounds

12 cups water

¼ cup bonito flakes
   (katsuobushi)

PREPARATION

Blanch the bones. Place the chicken carcass and pork bones in a stockpot and cover generously with cold water. Set the stockpot over high heat and bring to a boil. Boil for about 15 minutes. Drain the bones in a colander, discarding the water. Rinse the bones well.

STOVETOP METHOD

1. In a clean stockpot, combine the bones, kombu, pork belly, mushrooms, ginger, and water. Bring to a boil over high heat, skimming off any brown foam that rises to the top. Reduce the heat to low, add the bonito flakes, and simmer, uncovered, for 4 hours.

2. Using a colander, strain the broth. Cover and chill in the refrigerator for at least 4 hours.

3. When the broth is fully chilled, skim the fat off the top and save it to season your ramen (page 34).

PRESSURE COOKER METHOD

1. Place the bones in the pressure cooker and add the kombu, pork belly, mushrooms, ginger, and water. Cover and seal the pressure cooker and cook on high pressure for 1 hour. Quick release the pressure. Stir in the bonito flakes and let stand for 1 hour.

Continued

2. Using a colander, strain the broth. Cover and chill in the refrigerator for at least 4 hours.

3. When the broth is fully chilled, skim the fat off the top and save it to season your ramen (page 34).

Storage Tip: *Regardless of cooking method, you can store the broth, covered in the refrigerator for up to 1 week or in the freezer for up to 3 months.*

Repurposing Tip: *When you strain the solids from the broth, discard the bones but save the pork belly, which can be repurposed into a topping.*

AWASE DASHI

DAIRY-FREE, NUT-FREE

PREP TIME: 5 minutes / **COOK TIME:** 10 minutes

MAKES ABOUT 8 CUPS

Dashi is a common soup base, and there are numerous types, including kombu dashi (vegan, flavored with kelp), shiitake dashi (vegan, made by soaking dried shiitake mushrooms, page 26), niboshi dashi (flavored with dried anchovies), katsuo dashi (flavored with dried bonito flakes), and the most common, awase dashi, a "mixed" (*awase*) dashi.

2 (4-inch) squares kombu

8 cups water

4 cups dried bonito flakes

1. Make a few slits in the kombu to help it release its flavor.

2. Put the water and kombu in a medium saucepan. Set it over medium-low heat and bring almost to a boil. This will take about 10 minutes.

3. Remove the kombu. Raise the heat to medium and add the bonito flakes. Bring the mixture back up to a boil. Reduce the heat and simmer for about 30 seconds more, and then remove from the heat.

4. Let stand for 10 to 15 minutes, until the bonito flakes sink to the bottom of the pot. Strain through a fine-mesh sieve. Store the dashi in a covered container in the refrigerator for up to 1 week or in the freezer for up to 3 months.

Substitution Tip: *If you're short on time, you can find packets of instant dashi powder in Asian markets or the Asian foods aisle of most supermarkets that you can mix with water to use as a soup base.*

SHIITAKE DASHI

DAIRY-FREE, GLUTEN-FREE, NUT-FREE, VEGAN

PREP TIME: 5 minutes, plus overnight to steep

MAKES ABOUT 8 CUPS

Shiitake Dashi is one of the simplest dashis, and since it's made solely of shiitake mushrooms and water, it's the perfect base for vegan ramen. If you need it in a hurry, quickly steep the shiitakes in warm water for 30 minutes or so.

3 ounces dried shiitake
  mushrooms

8 cups water

1. Place the mushrooms in a large bowl or jar and cover with the water. Cover and refrigerate overnight.

2. Strain the liquid through a fine-mesh sieve, pressing on the solids to extract as much flavor as possible.

3. Store in a sealed container in the refrigerator for up to 1 week or in the freezer for up to 3 months.

Repurposing Tip: *Save the rehydrated mushrooms to use as a topping. Remove and discard the tough mushroom stems, then slice the mushrooms into strips.*

STEP 2: TARE

- **Miso Tare**
- **Spicy Miso Tare**

- **Shoyu Tare**
- **Shio Tare**

Unlike many soup stocks, ramen broth and seasoning are two separate elements. When you make ramen at home, you can make it quickly, but almost all "real" ramen cooks build ramen by layering broth(s) with tare and aromatic oils or fats.

Tare is the "secret sauce" that ramen cooks put at the bottom of your bowl. You can use the same broth for many different types of ramen and for other soups, but the tare gives each bowl its distinctive flavor. Each ramen shop and chef has their own secret tare recipes, and many are kept under lock and key.

Ichiran, a famous Japanese ramen chain that has a location in Brooklyn, is famous for their spicy red tare. Only four people in the world know how it's made and they are not allowed to travel on the same plane together. That's how tightly held some tare recipes are!

THE THREE MAIN TARE CATEGORIES ARE:

Miso
One of the essential tare elements, miso is a salty paste made from fermented soybeans and other grains. Miso tares are usually made from a blend of miso and other ingredients like mirin, sake, ginger, or soy sauce.

Shoyu (soy sauce)
This oldest and most traditional tare provides the concentrated flavor for shoyu ramen. It can be as simple as a blend of soy sauce, sake, and mirin, or include over a dozen ingredients, including kombu, chili peppers, and bonito flakes.

Shio (salt)
Shio tares are often believed to be just salt seasonings, but they are made from more than salt. They can be as simple as water, salt, and sake, but can also contain a complex layering of ingredients like kombu, shiitake mushrooms, sugar, mirin, sake, and bonito.

UMAMI

Umami, discovered and named by a Japanese chemist more than 100 years ago, is the fifth taste after sweet, sour, salty, and bitter. Generally used to describe foods that contain a high level of the amino acid glutamate, it imparts a savory, almost-meaty flavor. Seaweed, miso, mushrooms, preserved fish, ripe tomatoes, and fermented and aged foods like Parmesan cheese all contain high levels of glutamate. Using these umami-rich foods will impart a lot of flavor to your soups, sauces, dressings, and dishes.

SHOPPING LIST

You can find all these ingredients in Japanese and Asian grocery stores, and even your local grocery store might have key ingredients like soy sauce, mirin, and miso paste. Try to buy Japanese brands, if possible. You can also order ingredients online if you can't find what you need locally.

- **Brown sugar**
- **Chili paste or gochujang (Korean fermented chili paste)**
- **Dried shiitake mushrooms (or other high-quality dried mushrooms)**
- **Garlic**
- **Ginger**
- **Japanese sesame paste**

- **Kombu**
- **Kosher salt**
- **Mirin**
- **Miso, white and red**
- **Rice wine vinegar**
- **Sake**
- **Sesame oil**
- **Soy sauce**

EQUIPMENT LIST

Here are your tare essentials:

- **Measuring cups**
- **Measuring spoons**
- **Mixing bowls**
- **Saucepans**

- **Sharp knives**
- **Slotted spoons**
- **Storage containers**
- **Strainer**

These kitchen items are also nice to have:

- **Roasting pan**

- **Spice grinder or mortar and pestle**

PREPPING AND COOKING

Tare holds the ramen's essential flavor and often is used in a 1:10 part ratio in comparison with the broth, though this proportion is flexible based on how flavorful your tare is.

The most important aspect of tare is its combination of saltiness and umami. A simple shio tare can taste of salt, mirin, and kombu, while a simple shoyu tare might have the flavors of soy sauce, ginger, garlic, sake, and dried mushrooms. If your tare doesn't have as much depth as you'd like, focus on adding either umami (kelp, anchovy powder, fish sauce) or saltiness (miso, soy sauce, kosher salt) or both to your sauce, since these are the most important tastes that you need to flavor your broth.

Tare will keep for a few weeks in your refrigerator, and you can also use it as a stir-fry sauce or a dipping sauce for dumplings. In Japanese, the word "tare" actually means "dipping sauce."

MISO TARE

DAIRY-FREE, VEGAN

PREP TIME: 5 minutes

MAKES 1½ CUPS

Miso is a paste made of fermented soybeans and loaded with umami. To make a flavorful miso tare, the miso is combined with salt, Japanese sesame paste, sesame oil, and rice wine vinegar, resulting in a complex soup base. I like to combine mild, sweet white miso and more intense, umami-ful red miso for additional depth of flavor, but if you prefer, you can use just one or the other.

¼ cup white miso

¼ cup red miso

¼ cup kosher salt

¼ cup water

3 tablespoons Japanese sesame paste

2 tablespoons sesame oil

1 tablespoon rice wine vinegar

1. In a medium mixing bowl, combine the white and red miso, salt, water, Japanese sesame paste, sesame oil, and rice wine vinegar, and stir to mix well.

2. Store in an airtight container in the refrigerator for up to 3 weeks or in the freezer for up to 3 months.

Substitution Tip: *You can find Japanese sesame paste in Asian or Japanese markets. If you don't have it, substitute sesame tahini (or, in a pinch, you can use smooth, no-sugar-added peanut butter).*

SPICY MISO TARE

DAIRY-FREE, VEGAN

PREP TIME: 5 minutes

MAKES 2 CUPS

This mixture supplies a spicy kick along with the requisite umami. If you love spice, you'll want to make this tare in large batches and keep it on hand for any time you get a ramen craving. I especially love this tare combined with Clear Chicken Broth (page 17) and crispy Chicken Karaage (page 54).

⅓ cup chili paste or gochujang (Korean fermented chili paste)

¼ cup white miso

¼ cup red miso

¼ cup kosher salt

¼ cup water

3 tablespoons Japanese sesame paste

2 tablespoons sesame oil

1 tablespoon rice wine vinegar

1 tablespoon grated fresh ginger

1. In a medium mixing bowl, combine the chili paste, white and red miso, salt, water, Japanese sesame paste, sesame oil, rice wine vinegar, and ginger, and stir to mix well.

2. Store in an airtight container in the refrigerator for up to 3 weeks or in the freezer for up to 3 months.

Ingredient Tip: *Gochujang, another fermented product, adds yet another intense layer of umami. It can be found in Korean, Japanese, or Asian markets.*

SHOYU TARE

DAIRY-FREE, NUT-FREE, VEGAN

PREP TIME: 5 minutes / **COOK TIME:** 10 minutes

MAKES ABOUT 2 CUPS

Shoyu Tare starts with a base of soy sauce, but the other ingredients provide its seasoning depth and complexity. While the sake, mirin, and brown sugar bring acidity and sweetness, the garlic and ginger contribute aromatic flavor.

1 cup soy sauce

½ cup sake

½ cup mirin

1 tablespoon brown sugar

2 garlic cloves, smashed

1 (2-inch) piece ginger, peeled and cut into thick rounds

1. In a medium saucepan set over medium heat, combine the soy sauce, sake, mirin, brown sugar, garlic, and ginger, and bring to a simmer. Simmer for 10 minutes.

2. Strain the mixture through a fine-mesh sieve. Let cool and transfer to a 1-pint glass jar with a lid. Store in the refrigerator for up to 3 weeks or in the freezer for up to 3 months.

SHIO TARE

DAIRY-FREE, GLUTEN-FREE, NUT-FREE, VEGAN

PREP TIME: 5 minutes / **COOK TIME:** 1 hour

MAKES ABOUT 2 CUPS

"Shio" means "salt" in Japanese, but the taste of Shio Tare is far more complex than simple saltiness. Kombu and dried shiitake mushrooms provide layers of umami. This version is vegan, but niboshi (dried anchovies), bonito flakes, or fish sauce are sometimes added to create a depth of flavor to accompany the requisite saltiness.

1 cup water

1 cup sake

¼ cup mirin

1 (4-inch) piece kombu

1 ounce dried shiitake
  mushrooms

½ cup salt

1. In a medium saucepan, bring the water to a boil over high heat. Add the sake and mirin and simmer for 1 minute.

2. Reduce the heat to medium-low and add the kombu and shiitake mushrooms. Cover and gently simmer for 1 hour.

3. Add the salt to the pot and stir to dissolve. Remove from the heat and let cool to room temperature.

4. Strain through a fine-mesh sieve into an airtight container. Store in the refrigerator for up to 3 weeks or in the freezer for up to 3 months.

Repurposing Tip: *Use the reconstituted shiitake mushrooms as a ramen topping.*

STEP 3: AROMATIC OILS AND FAT

- **Rendered Chicken Fat**
- **Rendered Pork Fat**
- **Black Garlic Oil (*Mayu*)**
- **Chili Oil (*Rayu*)**
- **Scallion Oil**

A few drops or a generous drizzle of aromatic oil atop a bowl of ramen adds scent, body, flavor, and texture. Some ramen makers even say it makes slurping an easier task.

Most aromatic oils are made from fat that's flavored or infused with other ingredients. Garlic and onions are common aromatics. Ginger and chili peppers are frequent flavorings as well. You can use the fat you extract while making broth to make your aromatic oil, or you can use an unsaturated fat like vegetable oil. In some ramen-ya, a pat of butter takes the place of aromatic oil, and the effect is remarkably similar.

Mayu (black garlic oil) and *rayu* (chili oil) are two colorful and distinct oils. Mayu has a smoky, soft flavor, and is made from oil infused with blackened garlic, while the more common rayu is bright red thanks to chili peppers and spices.

SHOPPING LIST

You will be able to find almost all of these ingredients at your local grocery store. When cooking Japanese food, a neutral-flavored vegetable oil like grape-seed, sunflower, or canola works best. The *shichimi togarashi* is likely the only ingredient you will need to purchase at a specialty grocer or online. It's worth the extra effort, as the spice blend of chili peppers, orange peel, Japanese pepper, sesame seeds, ginger, and seaweed will add a unique spark to your ramen.

- **Garlic**
- **Ginger**
- **Ground cayenne pepper**
- **Chicken fat and skin, pork leaf or back fat, or reserved fat from making broth**
- **Scallions**
- **Sesame oil**
- **Shichimi togarashi**
- **Vegetable oil (grape-seed, sunflower, or canola)**

EQUIPMENT LIST

To create your aromatic oils and fat, you must have:

- **½-pint glass jars with lids (to store oils and fats)**
- **Blender**
- **Fine-mesh strainer or sieve**

- **Mixing bowls**
- **Saucepans**
- **Sauté pan or skillet**
- **Sharp knives**

PREPPING AND COOKING

The most basic aromatic oils consist of fat (animal or vegetable) infused or cooked with aromatics like ginger, garlic, and onions. For the purpose of crafting your ramen, you can use the fat you render while making your broth or a neutral-flavored vegetable oil.

You can also use these aromatic oils in other dishes, including cold noodle dishes, or as the oil component in a vinaigrette. Aromatic oils keep for at least 1 week in your refrigerator.

If the fat you render looks murky or you don't like the flavor of your oils, you can always use a pat of butter as your aromatic oil. It's a very common practice in Japan, and as butter has both fat and flavor, it adds a pleasing finish to your ramen.

RENDERED CHICKEN FAT

DAIRY-FREE, GLUTEN-FREE, NUT-FREE

PREP TIME: 5 minutes / **COOK TIME:** 1 hour

MAKES ABOUT 1 CUP

Rendered chicken fat (or any poultry fat, including duck or goose) makes a wonderful cooking fat. In Japan, it is used both as a cooking fat and as a topping. You can buy chicken fat to render at home, or get into the habit of trimming off excess fat and skin whenever you prepare chicken. Stash those scraps in a resealable plastic bag in the freezer until you have enough to make a jar of rendered fat. Rendered Chicken Fat can be used to make infused fats like Black Garlic Oil (page 38), Chili Oil (page 39), and Scallion Oil (page 40).

¾ pound chicken fat and skin, chopped

1. In a medium saucepan, place the chicken fat and skin and just barely cover with water. Set the pan over high heat and bring to a simmer. Reduce the heat to medium-low and simmer, stirring often, until the water has evaporated, the fat has liquefied, and the bits of skin have turned brown and become crisp, about 1 hour.

2. Strain through a fine-mesh sieve into a ½-pint glass jar with a lid. Rendered Chicken Fat can be stored in a jar in the refrigerator indefinitely.

Repurposing Tip: *Reserve the crispy bits of skin from the rendered fat, sprinkle them with salt, then add atop a bowl of ramen.*

RENDERED PORK FAT

DAIRY-FREE, GLUTEN-FREE, NUT-FREE

PREP TIME: 5 minutes / **COOK TIME:** 1 hour

MAKES ABOUT 1 CUP

Pork fat can be rendered using the same method as chicken fat. If you're making your own Tonkotsu, simply scrape off the fat that rises to the top after chilling the broth and store it to use in your ramen. With its high smoke point, rendered pork fat is also great for use in high-heat sautéing or stir-frying.

¾ pound pork leaf fat or back fat, chopped into small pieces or ground

1 cup water

1. In a medium saucepan, place the fat and a cup of water. Set the pan over high heat and bring to a simmer. Reduce the heat to medium-low and simmer, stirring often, until the water has evaporated, the fat has liquefied, and the little solid bits (cracklings) have begun to brown and settle to the bottom, about 1 hour.

2. Strain through a fine-mesh sieve into a ½-pint glass jar with a lid, reserving the cracklings for another use. Rendered Pork Fat can be stored in a jar in the refrigerator indefinitely. Store the reserved cracklings in a separate container in the refrigerator if you don't plan to use them immediately.

Ingredient Tip: *Pork leaf fat, the fat surrounding the pig's kidneys, is considered the "cleanest" fat and it's ideal for making rendered pork fat since it is pure white. Back fat (or fatback) can be used, but won't be as white or mild as leaf fat.*

BLACK GARLIC OIL (*MAYU*)

DAIRY-FREE, GLUTEN-FREE, NUT-FREE, VEGAN

PREP TIME: 10 minutes / **COOK TIME:** 30 minutes

MAKES ABOUT 1¼ CUPS

Mayu is an infused oil made by cooking garlic in a neutral-flavored oil until it turns completely black. The garlic and oil are puréed, resulting in a jet-black, bitter condiment. The flavor is intense and can be off-putting on its own, but when used sparingly it works magic on a bowl of ramen.

½ cup garlic cloves, peeled

½ cup neutral-flavored vegetable oil (such as sunflower or canola)

½ cup sesame oil

1. In a medium saucepan, place the garlic and vegetable oil and set it over medium-high heat. Cook, stirring often, until the garlic becomes very dark brown. This will take 20 to 30 minutes, but watch the pan carefully so the garlic doesn't burn. Remove the pan from the heat and let the mixture cool to room temperature. The garlic will continue to cook in the hot oil, so by the time it has cooled, the garlic should be black.

2. Transfer the mixture to a blender, add the sesame oil, and purée until smooth. Transfer the puréed mixture to a ½-pint glass jar and store, tightly covered, at room temperature for up to a week.

Ingredient Tip: *Black Garlic Oil is made with regular fresh garlic, not to be confused with fermented black garlic that you can buy in specialty markets.*

CHILI OIL (RAYU)

DAIRY-FREE, GLUTEN-FREE, NUT-FREE, SOY-FREE, VEGAN

PREP TIME: 10 minutes / **COOK TIME:** 5 minutes

MAKES ABOUT ½ CUP

Like mayu, rayu is an infused oil. This one is made by gently cooking garlic, ginger, scallion, and hot peppers in sesame oil before straining it. The result is spicy and layered, and a teaspoonful transforms a bowl of ramen.

½ cup sesame oil, divided

1 tablespoon minced fresh ginger

1 tablespoon minced garlic

1 scallion, white part only, finely minced

1 tablespoon shichimi togarashi

1 tablespoon ground cayenne pepper (optional)

1. In a small saucepan, combine ¼ cup of the sesame oil, ginger, garlic, and scallion and heat over medium-high heat until it simmers. Cook, stirring occasionally, reducing the heat as needed to keep it from boiling, for 3 minutes.

2. Remove the pan from the heat and transfer the mixture to a heat-safe bowl. Add the shichimi togarashi and the cayenne pepper, if using, and stir to combine. Let the mixture cool to room temperature.

3. Stir in the remaining ¼ cup of sesame oil.

4. Strain the mixture into a ½-pint glass jar. The oil can be stored in a jar in the refrigerator for up to 3 months.

Ingredient Tip: *Shichimi togarashi is a spice mix that contains seven seasonings including dried red chili pepper, dried citrus peel, sesame seeds, and sansho peppercorns. Find shichimi togarashi in the Asian foods aisle of most supermarkets or in Asian markets.*

SCALLION OIL

DAIRY-FREE, GLUTEN-FREE, NUT-FREE, VEGAN

PREP TIME: 5 minutes / **COOK TIME:** 1 hour

MAKES ABOUT 1 CUP

Scallion oil is simple to make and is great for adding the bright flavor of fresh herbs to a bowl of ramen. I make a batch of this any time I find myself with a bunch of extra scallions.

1 cup neutral-flavored vegetable oil

6 ounces scallions (about 3 bunches), trimmed and chopped into 2-inch pieces

1. In a medium saucepan, heat the oil over medium-high heat. Add the scallions and bring to a boil. Immediately reduce the heat to low and simmer for 45 to 50 minutes, stirring occasionally, until the scallions turn brown. Check the pan after 30 minutes.

2. Immediately strain the oil through a fine-mesh sieve into a glass jar. Press down gently on the solids in the sieve to release as much of the oil as you can. Store in a jar in the refrigerator for up to 3 months.

Repurposing Tip: *You can use scallion oil in place of your usual oil in other cooking. I love to toss it with fresh vegetables before roasting them or as a base for vinaigrette.*

STEP 4: NOODLES

- **Basic Ramen Noodles**
- **Gluten-Free Rice Noodles**

The most distinctive quality about ramen is the noodles and their familiar springy quality, with that unique mouthfeel, taste, and yellow hue. Although the standard ingredients of ramen noodles are the usual suspects of flour, salt, and water, there is one special ingredient that sets them apart: an alkaline solution called *kansui*. This lesser-known ingredient regulates the acidity when the noodles are made, and the alkaline water changes the dough's texture so that the noodles are firmer and better able to hold up in a hot soup.

Ramen noodles come in different widths and varieties to complement different broths. The most common categorization of ramen noodles refers to their alkalinity level, and they are generally characterized either as low alkaline (thin and straight) or high alkaline (wavy and springy). The alkaline level also affects the absorption rate of the broth.

Besides their alkalinity, ramen noodles are distinct thanks to their low water content. Each noodle's different hydration level also pairs best with different broths. If you'd like to go down a ramen rabbit hole, there is a whole science about which type of noodles pair best with varying soup bases. Briefly, drier noodles are perfect in tonkotsu ramens that are rich, thick, and less watery. Chewy or bouncier noodles pair better with shoyu or shio ramens made with clearer broths.

SHOPPING LIST

When shopping at a Japanese or Asian grocery store, kansui might be labeled as lye water, alkaline salt, or alkaline solution. Made from sodium carbonate (baking soda) and potassium carbonate, it might be hard to find if you don't have access to a good Japanese or Asian market, but you can easily make your own (see the Ingredient Tip on page 44).

- **00 flour**
- **Baking soda**
- **Bread flour**
- **Cornstarch**
- **Kansui**

- **Kosher salt**
- **Rice flour**
- **Vegetable oil (grape-seed, sunflower, or canola)**

EQUIPMENT LIST

Your must-have kitchen tools for noodle-making include:

- **8-inch baking dish**
- **Baking sheet**
- **Fine-mesh sieve**
- **Hand mixer**
- **Large mixing bowls**
- **Large stockpot**
- **Measuring cups**

- **Measuring spoons**
- **Mixing spoons**
- **Rolling pin**
- **Rubber spatula**
- **Sharp knife**
- **Wide saucepan with lid (or wok with a lid)**

The following items are nice to have, but not necessary:

- **Blender**
- **Noodle strainer/basket**

- **Pasta machine**
- **Stand mixer**

PREPPING AND COOKING

The ingredients for homemade ramen noodles are simple and easy to find everywhere (except for kansui, which you can find in most Asian groceries or online). If you can't find it, substitute with baked baking soda (see the Ingredient Tip on page 44).

Ramen noodles are essential to ramen. Use a different type of noodle and your noodle bowl is no longer ramen. Even some of the best ramen shops in America buy their noodles (most often from Sun Noodle, whose noodles are available at Whole Foods and other retailers). So, if you are not able to make your own, you shouldn't feel bad about buying good-quality ramen noodles.

If you can't find noodles at a store near you and you don't want to make them, you can transform regular pasta (spaghetti works well) to be springier and more ramen-like by adding 2 to 3 teaspoons of baking soda per quart of water while you are boiling your pasta.

BASIC RAMEN NOODLES

DAIRY-FREE, NUT-FREE, VEGAN

PREP TIME: 45 minutes, plus 1 hour to rest / **COOK TIME:** 1 minute

MAKES 8 SERVINGS

Ramen noodles are wheat flour noodles made with kansui powder, an alkalinizing agent that gives ramen noodles their unique springy texture and yellowish hue. The ratio of kansui powder to flour is what determines whether your noodles are thin and straight (low alkaline) or wavy and springy (high alkaline). This recipe is a strong starting point. Once you've mastered it, play around with using more or less kansui powder to create your own perfectly textured noodle.

1 cup cold water

1¼ teaspoons kansui powder

1½ teaspoons kosher salt

2 cups bread flour

2 cups plus 3 tablespoons 00 flour

Cornstarch, for dusting

1. In a small bowl, stir together the water and kansui powder until the powder dissolves. Add the salt and stir until the salt dissolves.

2. In the bowl of a stand mixer with the dough hook attached, combine the bread flour and 00 flour and, with the mixer running on low speed, slowly add the liquid. Continue to mix on low speed until a stiff dough forms, about 15 minutes. If it is too dry, add up to 2 tablespoons of additional cold water, 1 teaspoon at a time, until the dough comes together. If you don't have a stand mixer, you can make this dough by hand, but it will require some serious muscle. Stir together the wet and dry ingredients with a wooden spoon and then turn the dough out onto a lightly floured board. Knead by hand until the dough becomes quite stiff, about 25 to 30 minutes.

3. Turn the dough out from the stand mixer bowl onto a lightly floured countertop or cutting board and knead by hand for about 5 minutes more, until the dough becomes very stiff.

4. Place the dough in a clean bowl and cover with plastic wrap. Set aside to rest for 1 hour.

5. Line a baking sheet with parchment paper and dust it with a little cornstarch.

Continued

6. Split the dough into 8 balls of equal size. Sprinkle the balls with a little cornstarch and then flatten them into patties. Cover the dough balls with a sheet of plastic wrap while you work. Take one of the dough patties and roll it out as thin as you can with a rolling pin. Run the flattened dough through your pasta machine to press it to your desired thickness, dusting with cornstarch as needed to prevent sticking. Use the pasta machine to cut the noodles to your desired width. If you don't have a pasta machine, you can make the noodles by hand. Dust the rolling pin and work surface with a bit of cornstarch and roll each ball of dough into a very thin and even rectangle. Layer the cornstarch-dusted sheets on top of one another, trim the edges to make them straight, and then, using a large, very sharp knife, cut along the shorter edge into thin strips.

7. Toss the noodles with a bit of cornstarch and then set them in individual piles on the prepared baking sheet. (Each pile is 1 serving of noodles.)

8. To cook the noodles, bring a pot of salted water to a boil. Add the noodles and cook for 45 to 60 seconds for desired texture. Drain immediately.

9. To store, wrap each serving of noodles in plastic wrap or place in a resealable plastic bag. Store in the refrigerator for up to 5 days or in the freezer for up to 3 months. The noodles can be cooked straight from the refrigerator or freezer.

Ingredient Tip: *If you can't find kansui, make your own! Spread baking soda on a parchment-lined baking sheet and bake for 1 hour in a preheated 275°F oven. Let cool, then transfer the powder to a glass jar and store, covered, indefinitely.*

GLUTEN-FREE RICE NOODLES

DAIRY-FREE, GLUTEN-FREE, NUT-FREE, VEGAN

PREP TIME: 20 minutes, plus 30 minutes to rest / **COOK TIME:** 40 minutes

MAKES 8 SERVINGS

Noodles made with rice flour produce the best gluten-free substitute for wheat-based ramen noodles. If you make them wider and flatter, they can also be used in place of Thai-style rice noodles in dishes like pad thai.

2½ cups rice flour

¼ cup cornstarch

1 teaspoon kosher salt

2½ cups water

2 teaspoons neutral-flavored vegetable oil, divided, plus additional for brushing the noodle sheets

1. In a large mixing bowl, stir together the rice flour, cornstarch, salt, and water and combine well. Stir in 1 teaspoon of oil. Strain the mixture through a fine-mesh sieve into another bowl. Cover the bowl and let rest for 30 minutes at room temperature.

2. Fill a wide saucepan or wok (make sure an 8-inch baking pan fits inside) with water and bring to a boil. Reduce the heat to low, cover, and let the water simmer.

3. Coat the bottom of an 8-inch baking pan lightly with oil and pour ½ cup of the rice flour mixture into it, tilting the pan to cover the bottom completely in an even layer.

4. Float the pan in the simmering water and cover the saucepan with the lid. Add more water if needed to keep the baking pan afloat. Let it steam for 5 minutes.

5. Remove the lid and make sure there is still enough water in the saucepan (if not, add more). Brush the noodle sheet with oil and then pour another ½ cup of the rice flour mixture on top of the first, tilting the pan to cover evenly. Cover and steam for 5 minutes more.

6. Repeat with the remaining rice flour mixture (you'll get 7 or 8 noodle layers), steaming the last time for 8 minutes.

7. Line a baking sheet with parchment paper.

Continued

8. Brush a cutting board lightly with oil and then, using a rubber spatula, loosen the sides of the cooked noodle sheets and gently lift the whole stack of rice noodles out of the pan and onto the cutting board.

9. Use a very sharp knife to cut through the stack of noodle sheets to make noodles of your desired thickness. Toss the noodles to separate them and then form them into 8 noodle piles and place them on the prepared baking sheet. Cover with plastic wrap until ready to use.

10. These noodles taste best when used within a day or two of making them, but they can be frozen for longer storage. Wrap each noodle pile in plastic wrap or place in a resealable plastic bag and store in the refrigerator for up to 2 days or in the freezer for up to 3 months. To heat, pour very hot broth over the noodles.

Substitution Tip: *If you don't have rice flour, you can substitute 2½ cups long-grain rice soaked overnight in 2½ cups water. Process the soaked rice and water in a blender until very smooth, about 10 minutes, and then proceed with step 2.*

STEP 5: TOPPINGS

- **Chashu Pork Belly**
- **Ginger Pork**
- **Pork Katsu**
- **Chicken Chashu**
- **Chicken Karaage**
- **Soft-Boiled Eggs**
- **Soy Sauce Eggs**
- **Seasoned Bamboo Shoots (*Menma*)**
- **Red Pickled Ginger (*Beni Shoga*)**
- **Pickled Daikon Radish (Takuan)**
- **Roasted Kabocha Squash**
- **Roasted Tomatoes**

You can top your ramen with anything you like and, as the more than 10,000 ramen-ya in Japan can attest, there are seemingly endless possibilities to crown each bowl. The following recipes showcase some of the most traditional, beloved, and commonly seen cooked ramen toppings: chashu (braised pork slices), menma (preserved bamboo shoots), and eggs. The best ramen bowls have a combination of toppings, with the standouts boasting a variety of flavors and textures so that you get soft, crunchy, refreshing, savory, and sweet sensations all in one bowl.

Chashu, one of the most distinctive toppings, speaks to ramen's Chinese origins. An adaptation of the *char siu*, Chinese roasted barbecued pork, Japanese chashu is braised in sauce over low heat for hours. Although you can make chashu with different types of pork, it's become common to use pork belly.

SHOPPING LIST

Luckily, most of these ingredients are available in large chain grocery stores now.

- **Black pepper**
- **Brown sugar**
- **Chicken thighs**
- **Daikon radish**
- **Dashi**
- **Eggs**
- **Fresh bamboo shoots**
- **Garlic**
- **Ginger**
- **Ground pork**
- **Kabocha squash**
- **Kosher salt**
- **Mirin**
- **Olive oil**
- **Panko bread crumbs**
- **Plum tomatoes**
- **Pork belly**
- **Pork cutlets**
- **Potato starch**
- **Rice wine vinegar**
- **Sake**
- **Sesame oil**
- **Shoyu**
- **Soy sauce**

- **Star anise pods**
- **Sugar**
- **Turmeric**

- **Umezu or umeboshi vinegar**
- **Vegetable oil**
- **White miso**

EQUIPMENT LIST

Here are the items that you'll want to have handy in the kitchen as you create your ramen toppings:

- **Cast iron pan (or other oven-safe skillet) with lid**
- **Large sauté pan or skillet**
- **Large stockpot**
- **Measuring cups**

- **Measuring spoons**
- **Mixing bowls**
- **Saucepan**
- **Steamer**
- **Strainer**

PREPPING AND COOKING

If you are planning to make ramen, or having a ramen dinner party, you can (and should, for sanity's sake!) make almost all of your ramen components in the days leading up to your gathering. Almost all of the essential ingredients can be refrigerated or frozen, and even the noodles can be frozen, although you can make those fresh if you're nervous about reheating them. Because you can use all of your ramen components in other ways, it's wisest to make double or triple batches, guaranteeing they're available whenever a craving strikes. Chashu, for example, is wonderful when enjoyed over rice (*chashu don*), and you can incorporate both broth and tare as bases for countless other soups, stews, and sautéed dishes.

CHASHU PORK BELLY

DAIRY-FREE, NUT-FREE

PREP TIME: 15 minutes, plus overnight to chill / **COOK TIME:** 4 hours

SERVES 6 TO 8

Chashu Pork Belly is the quintessential ramen topping: skinless pork belly, rolled into a tight log and braised in a savory-sweet sauce that's infused with aromatics. Sliced into thin rounds and laid across a steaming bowl of ramen, it transforms a good bowl into a work of art.

1 (2- to 3-pound) slab skinless pork belly

¼ cup neutral-flavored vegetable oil

1 cup mirin

1 cup sake

1 cup soy sauce

¼ cup sugar

⅓ cup water

1 (3-inch) piece fresh ginger, peeled and sliced into thick rounds

2 star anise pods (optional)

1. Preheat the oven to 275°F.

2. Place the pork belly on a cutting board with the fat side down and then, starting with one of the long sides, roll it up into a tight cylinder or log. Use butcher's twine to tie the log, wrapping it at ½-inch intervals, securing the shape.

3. In a large, oven-safe skillet, heat the oil over high heat until it shimmers. Sear the pork belly on all sides until well-browned, about 8 minutes total.

4. In a saucepan, combine the mirin, sake, soy sauce, sugar, water, ginger, and star anise (if using). Bring to a boil over high heat and then pour the mixture over the meat in the skillet.

5. Cover the skillet loosely with a lid or aluminum foil and transfer it to the oven. Cook, turning occasionally, for 3 to 4 hours, until the pork is very tender and gives easily when you poke it with a fork or knife. Remove the skillet from the oven and transfer the meat and any juices to a heat-safe container. Let cool to room temperature, then cover and refrigerate overnight.

6. To serve, remove and discard the twine. With a very sharp knife, cut into thin slices.

Repurposing Tip: *Save the cooking liquid and use it as a marinade for a variation on Soy Sauce Eggs (page 56). Soft-boil 6 eggs, cool and peel them, then submerge them in the chilled chashu liquid. Marinate for 4 to 5 hours before serving.*

GINGER PORK

DAIRY-FREE, NUT-FREE

PREP TIME: 5 minutes / **COOK TIME:** 6 minutes

SERVES 4

For such a simple dish, this Ginger Pork topping is full of flavor. I make this in triple batches so that I can have it for multiple meals, whether on top of ramen or alongside rice.

1 pound ground pork

½ teaspoon salt

1 garlic clove, minced

1 (2-inch) piece fresh ginger, peeled and minced

1 teaspoon soy sauce

1. Heat a large skillet over medium-high heat. Add the pork and salt and cook, stirring occasionally and breaking up with a spatula, until the meat is browned, about 5 minutes.

2. Add the garlic and ginger and cook, stirring, for 1 minute more. Stir in the soy sauce and remove from the heat.

Substitution Tip: *Use any ground meat here: beef, turkey, chicken, or lamb.*

PORK KATSU

DAIRY-FREE, NUT-FREE

PREP TIME: 10 minutes / **COOK TIME:** 10 minutes

SERVES 4

To make Pork Katsu, thin pork cutlets are dipped in egg and coated in panko bread crumbs before being deep-fried. The end result is tender pork with a crispy, crunchy outer coating.

1 pound (¼-inch thick)
  pork cutlets
¾ teaspoon salt
¼ teaspoon freshly ground
  black pepper
Neutral-flavored vegetable oil,
  for deep-frying
1 large egg, lightly beaten
1 cup panko bread crumbs

1. Season the cutlets with the salt and pepper.

2. Fill a deep saucepan with about 3 inches of vegetable oil and heat over high heat until it shimmers.

3. Put the egg and panko in separate wide, shallow bowls. Dip the cutlets first into the egg and then into the bread crumbs, turning to coat well. Dip the coated pork into the egg a second time, and then coat with the bread crumbs again. Repeat with all the cutlets.

4. Gently lower each cutlet into the hot oil and cook for about 4 minutes, turning once at the 2-minute mark, until golden brown on both sides. Transfer the cooked cutlets to a paper towel–lined plate. Let the pork rest for 5 minutes or more and cut into thin strips.

Variation Tip: *This method can also be used for chicken breasts. Split 1 large chicken breast horizontally to make 2 fillets and then follow the instructions as written.*

CHICKEN CHASHU

DAIRY-FREE, NUT-FREE

PREP TIME: 15 minutes, plus 2 hours to marinate and overnight to chill / **COOK TIME:** 1 hour

SERVES 6 TO 8

This recipe applies the same cooking technique and flavors in Chashu Pork Belly (page 49) to boneless chicken thighs, which are marinated and then rolled together into a log wrapped in aluminum foil. Once it's steamed and chilled, slice the log just as you would the pork belly version.

¼ cup soy sauce

2 tablespoons sake

1 tablespoon sugar

2 teaspoons grated fresh ginger

2½ pounds skin-on, boneless chicken thighs

1. In a large bowl or resealable plastic bag, combine the soy sauce, sake, sugar, and ginger. Add the chicken and toss to coat. Cover or seal and marinate in the refrigerator for at least 2 hours or as long as overnight.

2. Remove the chicken from the marinade and arrange the pieces, skin side down, layered on top of each other to make a rectangle that is about 6 inches long and 3 inches wide on a large sheet of foil. Starting from one of the long sides of the rectangle, roll the chicken up into a tight log with the foil around the outside. Tie the log up with butcher's twine.

3. Set a steamer in a pot filled with a few inches of water and bring the water to a boil over high heat. Place the chicken in the steamer, cover the pot, and reduce the heat to low or medium-low. Steam for 1 hour, adding more water as needed. Remove the chicken from the steamer and let it cool for 30 minutes or so. Refrigerate overnight.

4. Remove the foil from the chicken and slice it thinly into rounds.

Ingredient Tip: *Use chicken thighs here rather than breasts. The thighs are higher in fat and are therefore less likely to dry out during cooking.*

CHICKEN KARAAGE

DAIRY-FREE, NUT-FREE

PREP TIME: 10 minutes, plus 30 minutes to marinate / **COOK TIME:** 5 minutes

SERVES 4

"Karaage" translates to "deep-fried" in English, and Chicken Karaage features juicy morsels of chicken marinated in soy sauce, sake, and seasonings, before being dredged in potato starch and double fried to give it an extra-crispy crust.

1 pound boneless, skinless chicken thighs, cut into 2-inch pieces

2 tablespoons soy sauce

1 tablespoon sake

1 teaspoon sesame oil

1 teaspoon grated fresh ginger

1 teaspoon sugar

Neutral-flavored vegetable oil, for deep-frying

½ cup potato starch

¼ teaspoon kosher salt

½ teaspoon freshly ground black pepper

1. Pat the chicken pieces dry with paper towels.

2. In a medium bowl, combine the soy sauce, sake, sesame oil, ginger, and sugar. Stir to mix. Add the chicken and toss to coat. Let marinate in the refrigerator for at least 30 minutes or as long as overnight.

3. Fill a deep saucepan with about 3 inches of vegetable oil (using a deep pot helps contain the splatter) and heat over high heat until it shimmers.

4. In a wide shallow bowl, stir together the potato starch, salt, and pepper. Lift the chicken pieces out of the marinade and dredge in the potato starch mixture, turning thoroughly to coat.

5. Gently lower the chicken pieces into the hot oil and cook until they are golden brown and float to the top, about 3 minutes, turning to ensure they brown all over. Transfer to a paper towel–lined plate and let cool for a few minutes before returning them to the oil to cook for another minute or so, until they are a deep golden brown. Transfer to another paper towel–lined plate to drain off excess oil.

Substitution Tip: *You can substitute boneless, skinless chicken breasts for the thighs.*

SOFT-BOILED EGGS

DAIRY-FREE, NUT-FREE, SOY-FREE, VEGETARIAN

PREP TIME: 5 minutes / **COOK TIME:** 6 minutes

MAKES 6 EGGS

It's one of the simplest of ramen toppings, but one that many ramen lovers consider essential—a perfectly cooked egg with its white just set, concealing a jammy, brightly colored yolk in the center. These soft-boiled eggs are easy to prepare, requiring just a few simple tricks and a keen eye on the timer to achieve perfection, but once in the bowl they're unforgettably delicious.

6 large eggs, at room temperature

1. With a pin, make a small hole in the rounded bottom of each egg.

2. Fill a large saucepan with water and bring to a boil over high heat. Reduce the heat to medium so that the water is at a hard simmer. Gently lay the eggs in the water using a spoon. For the first 2 minutes, use chopsticks to spin the eggs around gently in a circle. This helps the yolk set in the center of the white part, making for a nicer presentation.

3. Let simmer for 4 more minutes.

4. While the eggs are simmering, prepare an ice water bath in a large bowl big enough to comfortably hold the eggs.

5. When the eggs are finished cooking, drain them first, then run cold water over them to cool them down quickly. Transfer the eggs to the ice water bath and let them sit for about 5 minutes, until they are completely chilled. Remove the eggs from the ice water bath and refrigerate until ready to use. Unpeeled eggs will keep in the refrigerator for up to 5 days.

6. To serve the soft-boiled eggs, carefully peel them and slice them in half lengthwise. Float 1 or 2 halves on top of a bowl of ramen.

Repurposing Tip: *Use the soft-boiled eggs to make Soy Sauce Eggs (page 56).*

SOY SAUCE EGGS

DAIRY-FREE, NUT-FREE, VEGETARIAN

PREP TIME: 5 minutes, plus 10 hours to marinate / **COOK TIME:** 4 minutes

MAKES 6 EGGS

A perfectly cooked Soft-Boiled Egg (page 55) is a delightful topping, but gets even better once the egg is pickled in a brine made of soy sauce and sake. Once you've soft-boiled a bunch of eggs, it takes just a few more minutes and a bit more effort to turn them into Soy Sauce Eggs, subtly flavored with the Japanese-style soy sauce called shoyu, sake, mirin, ginger, and a touch of sugar.

¾ cup shoyu or low-sodium soy sauce

½ cup sake

¼ cup mirin

¾ cup warm water

1 tablespoon sugar

2 teaspoons chopped fresh ginger

6 Soft-Boiled Eggs (page 55), chilled and peeled

1. In a saucepan, combine the shoyu, sake, mirin, water, sugar, and ginger. Bring to a boil over high heat, then reduce to medium-low and simmer, stirring frequently, until the sugar is completely dissolved, about 3 to 4 minutes. Transfer to a jar or container large enough to fit both the eggs and the liquid, and let cool.

2. Add the peeled eggs to the cooled shoyu mixture and let marinate in the refrigerator for 8 to 10 hours (no longer than 12 hours or the eggs will become rubbery). Remove the eggs from the marinade and keep them in a bowl or jar, covered, in the refrigerator until ready to use. The eggs will keep in the refrigerator for up to 3 days.

3. To serve, slice the eggs in half lengthwise and float 1 or 2 halves on top of a bowl of ramen.

Repurposing Tip: *Beyond the ramen bowl, Soy Sauce Eggs make a great snack and they're an excellent protein to pack in a lunch box.*

SEASONED BAMBOO SHOOTS (*MENMA*)

DAIRY-FREE, NUT-FREE

PREP TIME: 5 minutes / **COOK TIME:** 20 minutes

MAKES ABOUT 2 CUPS

Menma are among the most popular toppings, slightly sweet with a nice crunch. This version is made by braising fresh bamboo shoots in a seasoned broth.

2 cups dashi

1 tablespoon sesame oil

1 tablespoon soy sauce

1 tablespoon sake

1 tablespoon sugar

1 teaspoon kosher salt

1 pound fresh bamboo shoots, halved lengthwise and cut into strips

1. In a large saucepan, stir together the dashi, sesame oil, soy sauce, sake, sugar, and salt. Add the bamboo shoots and bring to a boil over high heat.

2. Reduce the heat to medium and cook, uncovered, for 20 minutes, or until most of the liquid is gone.

3. Serve immediately or store in the refrigerator for up to a week or in the freezer for up to 3 months.

Ingredient Tip: *The flavor difference between fresh and canned shoots is vast. If you can't find fresh bamboo shoots, look for jarred fermented ones rather than substituting canned.*

RED PICKLED GINGER (*BENI SHOGA*)

DAIRY-FREE, GLUTEN-FREE, NUT-FREE, VEGAN

PREP TIME: 10 minutes, plus 2 weeks to pickle

MAKES ABOUT 2 CUPS

Beni Shoga is julienned ginger that has been pickled in umezu, the vinegary liquid that's created during the pickling process of Japanese plums (umeboshi). Red shiso leaves from the umezu brine turn the vinegar red, which in turn colors the ginger.

1 cup umezu or umeboshi
   vinegar

2 tablespoons kosher salt

2 tablespoons sugar

¼ cup mirin

½ pound fresh ginger, peeled
   and cut into 2-inch-long
   matchstick pieces

1. In a glass bowl or jar, combine the umezu or umeboshi vinegar, salt, sugar, and mirin. Add the ginger, cover, and refrigerate for at least 2 weeks.

2. Beni shoga will keep in a covered jar in the refrigerator indefinitely.

Ingredient Tip: *You can find umezu or umeboshi vinegar in Japanese or Asian markets, and find jarred beni shoga there as well.*

PICKLED DAIKON RADISH (*TAKUAN*)

DAIRY-FREE, GLUTEN-FREE, NUT-FREE, VEGAN

PREP TIME: 10 minutes, plus 2 hours to drain and 2 days to cure / **COOK TIME:** 5 minutes

MAKES ABOUT 1 PINT

Takuan is a fermented daikon radish pickle that takes months to prepare. If you prefer something homemade but don't want to wait months, this "quick" pickled daikon radish is ready in just 2 days. It adds a crisp, refreshing contrast to a rich, meaty bowl of ramen.

1 daikon radish, peeled and sliced into thin rounds

1 tablespoon salt

½ cup sugar

½ cup water

½ cup rice wine vinegar

1 teaspoon ground turmeric

1. Toss the daikon rounds with the salt and let stand in a colander (set over a bowl or in the sink) for about 2 hours.

2. In a medium saucepan over medium-high heat, combine the sugar, water, rice wine vinegar, and turmeric and bring to a boil. Cook, stirring, until the sugar dissolves, about 3 minutes.

3. Squeeze any excess water from the daikon and transfer to a heat-safe jar or bowl. Pour the hot pickling liquid over the top. Cover and refrigerate for at least 2 days.

4. Pickled Daikon Radish will keep in the refrigerator for at least 1 month.

Repurposing Tip: *Pickled Daikon Radish also makes a great vegan filling for Japanese rice balls (onigiri) or an accompaniment for a bowl of steamed rice.*

ROASTED KABOCHA SQUASH

DAIRY-FREE, NUT-FREE, VEGAN

PREP TIME: 5 minutes / **COOK TIME:** 30 minutes

SERVES 4

Kabocha squash is a Japanese pumpkin with a velvety texture and sweet flavor, especially when roasted. Tossing it with an umami-loaded mixture of miso and soy sauce intensifies the flavors even further, making it an ideal topping for a vegetarian or vegan ramen.

1 tablespoon white miso

2 teaspoons soy sauce

1 tablespoon neutral-flavored vegetable oil

2 teaspoons brown sugar

½ kabocha squash, peeled, seeded, and cut into cubes

1. Preheat the oven to 400°F.

2. In a medium bowl, stir together the miso, soy sauce, oil, and brown sugar to combine well. Add the squash and toss to coat.

3. Spread the squash out in a single layer on a baking sheet and roast in the oven for 25 to 30 minutes, until tender and beginning to brown.

Ingredient Tip: *You can find kabocha squash in Asian markets and some supermarkets or farmers' markets. If you can't find it, feel free to substitute sugar pumpkin or butternut squash.*

OTHER TOPPINGS

These ramen toppings don't require full recipes, but they are some of the most common accompaniments you'll find around the world. Some add a fresh crunch, others add a creamy depth, and still others bring a bright sweetness.

Bean sprouts

Butter

Corn

Greens (like spinach or mustard greens)

Japanese mushrooms (wood ear, shiitake)

Kamaboko (a fish cake)

Onions

Scallions or *negi* (Japanese leeks)

Seaweed

ROASTED TOMATOES

DAIRY-FREE, GLUTEN-FREE, NUT-FREE, VEGAN

PREP TIME: 5 minutes / **COOK TIME:** 30 minutes

SERVES 4

Ivan Orkin made a splash by using roasted tomatoes as a ramen topping. It's a surprising ingredient in Japanese cuisine since tomatoes aren't native to the country, but their addition to the ramen arsenal is a stroke of genius. When added to the bowl, they bring umami and luscious texture.

12 plum tomatoes, halved lengthwise, cored and seeded

4 tablespoons extra-virgin olive oil

1½ teaspoons kosher salt

½ teaspoon freshly ground black pepper

1. Preheat the oven to 450°F.

2. In a large bowl, toss the tomatoes with olive oil to coat well. Arrange the tomatoes cut-side up on a baking sheet and sprinkle them with salt and pepper.

3. Roast until the tomatoes are very soft and starting to caramelize around the edges, about 30 minutes. Remove from the oven.

4. Roasted tomatoes will keep, in a covered container in the refrigerator, for up to 1 week.

Repurposing Tip: *Roasted tomatoes make a great side for roasted meat or fish and a delicious topping for plain steamed rice.*

STEP 6: THE BOWL

Once you have all of your components made, the fun begins. Assembling the bowl lets you showcase your culinary creations. Here, you will master what it takes to pull together a restaurant-worthy bowl of ramen.

A perfect bowl of ramen is bursting with layers of flavor and texture, but it's not hard to assemble once you have made all the elements involved. Ramen includes a lot of different components, but since you did the work in advance, assembling the bowl itself mostly takes smart timing and organization.

Truly, timing is everything when assembling your bowl of ramen because the goal is to enjoy your ramen piping hot! Slurping is acceptable (even encouraged!) in ramen shops in Japan because it makes it easier for you to enjoy the noodles while they are hot (as you slurp your noodles in, you also inhale air, helping to cool the noodles and broth). So even though I highly recommend making most of your ramen essentials a day or two in advance to spread out the work, you still need to be organized so that your broth, noodles, and toppings are hot at the same time.

EQUIPMENT LIST

Ramen requires nothing special for serving except for extremely large soup bowls. The piping-hot broth, stack of noodles, and toppings are best enjoyed in a wide, deep bowl. It's almost inevitable to splash a bit while slurping, and a deeper bowl helps keep it contained. When sourcing your bowls, it is worth going to an Asian market or buying online, as you probably won't be able to find non-Asian soup bowls at this size.

- **Large soup bowls**
- **Large stockpots**
- **Measuring cups**
- **Measuring spoons**
- **Noodle basket or strainer**

PREPPING AND ASSEMBLING

- Set your toppings, tare, and aromatic oil in separate bowls on your counter.
- Set your ramen bowls in front of your toppings.
- Place one tablespoon of tare at the bottom of each ramen bowl (or more or less, depending on your recipe).
- Set a pot of water to boil for your noodles.
- In another pot, heat the broth over high heat until small bubbles form around the edge and it is just about to boil, then simmer until you are ready to use it.
- Once your noodle water is boiling, boil your ramen noodles (1 minute for fresh and 2 to 3 minutes for packaged).
- Once your noodles are done, strain them and shake them vigorously to remove excess water.
- Ladle hot ramen broth into your bowl.
- Add a handful of cooked ramen noodles to the broth.
- Add your aromatic oil—a few drops to a drizzle, depending on your taste.
- Finish with the rest of your toppings.
- Serve while it is still piping hot.

Japanese Regional Ramen

Tonkotsu Ramen

Shoyu Ramen

Shio Ramen

Miso Ramen

Other Ramen

Sides

PART III

THE RECIPES

HAKATA-STYLE MOUNTAIN OF SCALLIONS RAMEN, PAGE 83

JAPANESE REGIONAL RAMEN

SAPPORO RAMEN

NUT-FREE

PREP TIME: 15 minutes / **COOK TIME:** 15 minutes

SERVES 4

Located on Hokkaido, the northernmost of Japan's islands, Sapporo is known for its brisk winters, so it's fitting that the local ramen employs a hearty kotteri (thick and oily) broth with rich Miso Tare. Sapporo ramen is satisfyingly topped with Chashu Pork Belly, Seasoned Bamboo Shoots, sweet corn, and butter.

½ cup Miso Tare (page 30) or Spicy Miso Tare (page 31)

8 cups Tonkotsu (page 21)

1 tablespoon neutral-flavored vegetable oil

12 slices Chashu Pork Belly (page 49)

2 tablespoons unsalted butter

1 cup fresh corn kernels, cut from one large ear of corn

18 ounces Basic Ramen Noodles (page 43 or store-bought) or 12 ounces dried ramen noodles

Seasoned Bamboo Shoots (page 57)

1. Spoon 2 tablespoons of the tare into each of 4 serving bowls.

2. In a large saucepan, heat the Tonkotsu over high heat until small bubbles form around the edge and it is just about to boil.

3. While the broth is heating, heat the vegetable oil in a skillet and warm the pork slices in it for 1 to 2 minutes on each side. Once the pork has been heated, remove from the skillet and set aside.

4. Add the butter to the skillet. When the butter is melted and bubbling, add the corn kernels and cook, stirring frequently, for about 2 minutes, until the edges just begin to brown.

5. Cook the noodles according to the recipe (or package instructions) and drain well.

6. When the noodles are done cooking, immediately ladle the hot soup into the serving bowls over the tare. Add ¼ of the noodles to each bowl. Stir gently and lift with chopsticks to distribute the tare into the broth and to coat the noodles. The noodles should float on top somewhat.

7. Top each bowl with 3 slices of pork, a few spoonfuls of corn, and some bamboo shoots. Serve immediately.

Substitution Tip: *If you don't have fresh corn on the cob, substitute frozen corn kernels. Add them, while still frozen, to the melted butter in the hot pan. They'll thaw and heat quickly.*

HAKODATE RAMEN

DAIRY-FREE, NUT-FREE

PREP TIME: 15 minutes / **COOK TIME:** 15 minutes

SERVES 4

Shio ramen (seasoned with salty tare) is the type for which Hakodate is famous. The pork or chicken broth is assari (light) and the noodles are thin and straight. The basic toppings are Chashu Pork Belly, Seasoned Bamboo Shoots, scallions, bean sprouts, and Soft-Boiled Eggs. Because Hakodate is a port city, seaweed and seafood are often incorporated.

½ cup Shio Tare (page 33)

8 cups Clear Chicken Broth (page 17)

1 tablespoon neutral-flavored vegetable oil

12 slices Chashu Pork Belly (page 49)

18 ounces Basic Ramen Noodles (page 43 or store-bought) or 12 ounces dried ramen noodles

¼ cup sliced scallions, green and white parts

½ cup bean sprouts

Seasoned Bamboo Shoots (page 57)

1 sheet nori (seaweed), cut into strips about 3 inches long and ½ inch wide

2 Soft-Boiled Eggs (page 55), halved lengthwise

1. Spoon 2 tablespoons of the tare into each of 4 serving bowls.

2. In a large saucepan, heat the Clear Chicken Broth over high heat until small bubbles form around the edge and it is just about to boil.

3. While the broth is heating, heat the vegetable oil in a skillet and warm the pork slices in it for 1 to 2 minutes on each side.

4. Cook the noodles according to the recipe (or package instructions) and then drain well.

5. When the noodles are done cooking, immediately ladle the hot soup into the serving bowls over the tare. Add ¼ of the noodles to each bowl. Stir gently and lift with chopsticks to distribute the tare into the broth and to coat the noodles. The noodles should float on top somewhat.

6. Top each bowl with 3 slices of pork, ¼ of the scallions, bean sprouts, bamboo shoots, and nori. Float half of 1 egg in each bowl. Serve immediately.

Prep-Ahead Tip: *All of these ramen ingredients can be made 2 or 3 days ahead of time and kept in the refrigerator. Let the eggs and bamboo shoots come to room temperature before serving.*

ASAHIKAWA RAMEN

DAIRY-FREE, NUT-FREE

PREP TIME: 15 minutes / **COOK TIME:** 15 minutes

SERVES 4

Asahikawa is a destination for ramen lovers. There's even a "ramen village" where eight famous ramen shops opened outposts, forming their own ramen mini-mall. Asahikawa's traditional ramen is seasoned with Shoyu Tare and uses a "double broth," a combination of Tonkotsu and fish-based dashi. Known as a hub for the seafood that's transported throughout the island, as well as for its pork farms, the city's local food products shine in these steaming bowls.

½ cup Shoyu Tare (page 32)

4 cups Tonkotsu (page 21)

4 cups Awase Dashi (page 25)

4 dried wood ear mushrooms, rinsed and dried

1 tablespoon neutral-flavored vegetable oil

12 slices Chashu Pork Belly (page 49)

18 ounces Basic Ramen Noodles (page 43 or store-bought) or 12 ounces dried ramen noodles

Seasoned Bamboo Shoots (page 57)

1. Spoon 2 tablespoons of the tare into each of 4 serving bowls.

2. In a large saucepan, combine the Tonkotsu and Awase Dashi and heat over high heat until small bubbles form around the edge and it is just about to boil.

3. Place the wood ear mushrooms in a small bowl and pour boiling water over them to cover. Let them sit for about 10 minutes, and then drain and cut them into strips.

4. While the broth is heating, heat the vegetable oil in a skillet and warm the pork slices in it for 1 to 2 minutes on each side.

5. Cook the noodles according to the recipe (or package instructions) and then drain well.

6. When the noodles are done cooking, immediately ladle the hot soup into the serving bowls over the tare. Add ¼ of the noodles to each bowl. Stir gently and lift with chopsticks to distribute the tare into the broth and to coat the noodles. The noodles should float on top somewhat.

7. Top each bowl with 3 slices of pork, 1 mushroom, and some bamboo shoots. Serve immediately.

Ingredient Tip: *Dried wood ear mushrooms, a wide and thin fungus, are sold in Asian markets or the Asian foods aisle of many supermarkets. Their flavor is mild, but they add a nice crunch.*

KITAKATA RAMEN

DAIRY-FREE, NUT-FREE

PREP TIME: 15 minutes, plus overnight to refrigerate / **COOK TIME:** 1 hour and 5 minutes

SERVES 4

The small city of Kitakata in Fukushima opened its first ramen shop in 1926. Many city residents are so fond of the dish they eat it for breakfast! Kitakata-style is a "double soup" ramen combining either pork or chicken broth with a fish-based broth (usually made with dried anchovies) and simple toppings.

FOR THE NIBOSHI DASHI

5 cups water

3 ounces niboshi (dried anchovies)

1 (3-inch) square of kombu

½ ounce bonito flakes

FOR THE RAMEN

½ cup Shio Tare (page 33)

4 cups Tonkotsu (page 21) or Clear Chicken Broth (page 17)

1 tablespoon neutral-flavored vegetable oil

12 slices Chashu Pork Belly (page 49)

18 ounces Basic Ramen Noodles (page 43 or store-bought) or 12 ounces dried ramen noodles

Seasoned Bamboo Shoots (page 57)

¼ cup sliced scallions, green and white parts

2 Soft-Boiled Eggs (page 55) halved lengthwise

¼ cup Rendered Chicken Fat (page 36)

TO MAKE THE NIBOSHI DASHI

1. In a large bowl or stockpot, combine the water, niboshi, and kombu and refrigerate it overnight.

2. Bring the mixture to a bare simmer over medium heat, just until small bubbles begin to form and float to the top of the pot. Remove the piece of kombu and raise the temperature to medium-high. Simmer, uncovered, for 40 minutes.

3. Add the bonito flakes and let simmer for 10 minutes more.

4. Strain the broth through a fine-mesh sieve.

TO MAKE THE RAMEN

1. Spoon 2 tablespoons of the Shio Tare into each of 4 serving bowls.

2. In a large saucepan, combine the niboshi dashi and the broth. Heat over high heat until small bubbles form around the edge and it is just about to boil.

3. While the broth is heating, heat the vegetable oil in a skillet and warm the pork slices in it for 1 to 2 minutes on each side.

4. Cook the noodles according to the recipe (or package instructions) and then drain well.

Continued

5. When the noodles are done cooking, immediately ladle the hot soup into the serving bowls over the tare. Add ¼ of the noodles to each bowl. Stir gently and lift with chopsticks to distribute the tare into the broth and to coat the noodles. The noodles should float on top somewhat.

6. Top each bowl with 3 slices of pork, bamboo shoots, scallions, half of 1 egg, and a spoonful of the chicken fat. Serve immediately.

HAKATA RAMEN

DAIRY-FREE, NUT-FREE

PREP TIME: 15 minutes / **COOK TIME:** 15 minutes

SERVES 4

Thick, milky Tonkotsu rules Hakata's ramen scene. Shio Tare is the most common seasoning base, but you'll also find miso and shoyu variations. Chashu Pork Belly is a popular topping, along with Red Pickled Ginger (Beni Shoga). Garlicky sautéed mustard greens add pungent flavor.

FOR THE MUSTARD GREENS

1 tablespoon neutral-flavored vegetable oil

2 garlic cloves, peeled and minced

1 pound mustard greens, cut into ribbons

¼ teaspoon kosher salt

¼ teaspoon freshly ground black pepper

¼ teaspoon sesame oil

FOR THE RAMEN

½ cup Shio Tare (page 33)

8 cups Tonkotsu (page 21)

1 tablespoon neutral-flavored vegetable oil

12 slices Chashu Pork Belly (page 49)

18 ounces Basic Ramen Noodles (page 43 or store-bought) or 12 ounces dried ramen noodles

¼ cup Red Pickled Ginger (page 58)

TO MAKE THE MUSTARD GREENS

1. In a large skillet, heat the oil over medium-high heat until it shimmers. Add the garlic and greens and cook, stirring frequently, until the greens begin to wilt.

2. Add the salt and pepper and continue to cook, stirring frequently (add a few tablespoons of water if needed to prevent greens from sticking or burning), until the greens are wilted, 3 to 5 minutes. Remove from the heat and stir in the sesame oil.

TO MAKE THE RAMEN

1. Spoon 2 tablespoons of the Shio Tare into each of 4 serving bowls.

2. In a large saucepan, heat the Tonkotsu over high heat until small bubbles form around the edge and it is just about to boil.

3. While the broth is heating, heat the vegetable oil in a skillet and warm the pork slices in it for 1 to 2 minutes on each side.

4. Cook the noodles according to the recipe (or package instructions) and then drain well.

5. When the noodles are done cooking, immediately ladle the hot soup into the serving bowls over the tare. Add ¼ of the noodles to each bowl. Stir gently and lift with chopsticks to distribute the tare into the broth and to coat the noodles. The noodles should float on top somewhat.

Continued

6. Top each bowl with 3 slices of pork, ¼ of the Red Pickled Ginger, and ¼ of the prepared mustard greens. Serve immediately.

Substitution Tip: *Mustard greens add a spicy quality. If you can't find them, substitute another hearty green like Swiss chard or kale, and add freshly ground pepper to create some spiciness.*

TOKYO RAMEN

DAIRY-FREE, NUT-FREE

PREP TIME: 15 minutes / **COOK TIME:** 15 minutes

SERVES 4

Japan's capital city is home to countless types of ramen, but its signature bowl is a shoyu ramen made with a double broth of chicken and dashi. The wavy noodles tend toward a chewy consistency, and common toppings include bean sprouts, chopped scallions, Soft-Boiled Eggs, Chashu Pork Belly, and kamaboko (a sliced fish cake).

½ cup Shoyu Tare (page 32)

4 cups Clear Chicken Broth (page 17)

4 cups Awase Dashi (page 25)

1 tablespoon neutral-flavored vegetable oil

12 slices Chashu Pork Belly (page 49)

18 ounces fresh wavy ramen noodles (store-bought)

12 slices kamaboko

½ cup bean sprouts

¼ cup chopped scallions, green and white parts

2 Soft-Boiled Eggs (page 55)

1. Spoon 2 tablespoons of the tare into each of 4 serving bowls.

2. In a large saucepan, combine the Clear Chicken Broth and Awase Dashi and heat over high heat until small bubbles form around the edge and it is just about to boil.

3. While the broth is heating, heat the vegetable oil in a skillet and warm the pork slices in it for 1 to 2 minutes on each side.

4. Cook the noodles according to the recipe (or package instructions) and then drain well.

5. When the noodles are done cooking, immediately ladle the hot soup into the serving bowls over the tare. Add ¼ of the noodles to each bowl. Stir gently and lift with chopsticks to distribute the tare into the broth and to coat the noodles. The noodles should float on top somewhat.

6. Top each bowl with 3 slices of pork, 3 slices of kamaboko, ¼ of the bean sprouts, 1 tablespoon of scallions, and half of 1 soft-boiled egg. Serve immediately.

Ingredient Tip: *Kamaboko is a cake made by puréeing white fish, pressing it into a loaf, and steaming it until firm. Find kamaboko in the freezer sections of Asian markets, and in some supermarkets.*

WAKAYAMA CHUKA SOBA

DAIRY-FREE, NUT-FREE

PREP TIME: 15 minutes / **COOK TIME:** 15 minutes

SERVES 4

Wakayama, a region known for its soy sauce, is home to Ide Shoten, one of the best ramen shops in all of Japan. Wakayama ramen is seasoned with Shoyu Tare. The noodles are usually thin and straight, with toppings like Chashu Pork Belly, Seasoned Bamboo Shoots, and scallions. Ramen shops often serve the local specialty hayazushi (leaf-wrapped mackerel sushi) and Soft-Boiled Eggs alongside their bowls of ramen.

½ cup Shoyu Tare (page 32)

8 cups Tonkotsu (page 21)

1 tablespoon neutral-flavored vegetable oil

12 slices Chashu Pork Belly (page 49)

18 ounces Basic Ramen Noodles (page 43 or store-bought) or 12 ounces dried ramen noodles

½ cup Seasoned Bamboo Shoots (page 57)

½ cup bean sprouts

¼ cup chopped scallions, green and white parts

1. Spoon 2 tablespoons of the tare into each of 4 serving bowls.

2. In a large saucepan, heat the Tonkotsu over high heat until small bubbles form around the edge and it is just about to boil.

3. While the broth is heating, heat the vegetable oil in a skillet and warm the pork slices in it for 1 to 2 minutes on each side.

4. Cook the noodles according to the recipe (or package instructions) and then drain well.

5. When the noodles are done cooking, immediately ladle the hot soup into the serving bowls over the tare. Add ¼ of the noodles to each bowl. Stir gently and lift with chopsticks to distribute the tare into the broth and to coat the noodles. The noodles should float on top somewhat.

6. Top each bowl with 3 slices of pork, ¼ of the Seasoned Bamboo Shoots, ¼ of the bean sprouts, and 1 tablespoon of scallions. Serve immediately.

KYOTO RAMEN

DAIRY-FREE, NUT-FREE

PREP TIME: 15 minutes / **COOK TIME:** 15 minutes

SERVES 4

Kyoto is famous for delicate kaiseki cuisine, yet the ramen here is rich, thick, and bold. Although shoyu is the usual seasoning, the broth can be a thick chicken broth or a combination broth made from chicken, pork, and seafood. Common toppings are Chashu Pork Belly, chopped scallions, Seasoned Bamboo Shoots, nori, and sometimes a spoonful of Rendered Pork Fat or a pat of butter.

½ cup Shoyu Tare (page 32)

8 cups Pork and Chicken Broth (page 23)

1 tablespoon neutral-flavored vegetable oil

12 slices Chashu Pork Belly (page 49)

18 ounces Basic Ramen Noodles (page 43 or store-bought) or 12 ounces dried ramen noodles

4 teaspoons of Rendered Pork Fat (page 37) or butter

½ cup Seasoned Bamboo Shoots (page 57)

¼ cup chopped scallions, green and white parts

1 nori sheet, cut into 3-inch ribbons

1. Spoon 2 tablespoons of the tare into each of 4 serving bowls.

2. In a large saucepan, heat the Pork and Chicken Broth over high heat until small bubbles form around the edge and it is just about to boil.

3. While the broth is heating, heat the vegetable oil in a skillet and warm the pork slices in it for 1 to 2 minutes on each side.

4. Cook the noodles according to the recipe (or package instructions) and then drain well.

5. When the noodles are done cooking, immediately ladle the hot soup into the serving bowls over the tare. Add ¼ of the noodles to each bowl. Stir gently and lift with chopsticks to distribute the tare into the broth and to coat the noodles. The noodles should float on top somewhat.

6. Top each bowl with 1 teaspoon of the Pork Fat or butter, 3 slices of pork, ¼ of the Seasoned Bamboo Shoots, 1 tablespoon of scallions, and ¼ of the nori. Serve immediately.

TAKAYAMA RAMEN

DAIRY-FREE, NUT-FREE

PREP TIME: 15 minutes / **COOK TIME:** 25 minutes

SERVES 4

In Takayama, ramen broth is usually a mixture of chicken broth, dashi, and soy sauce. Although most ramen shops use tare to flavor the broth, in Takayama it is more common to boil the seasoning ingredients together with the broth. Takayama Ramen, or Chuka soba, is bold in flavor but restrained in toppings.

1 tablespoon sesame oil

1 tablespoon minced fresh ginger

2 garlic cloves, minced

6 cups Clear Chicken Broth (page 17)

2 cups Awase Dashi (page 25)

1 leek, white part only, halved lengthwise and thinly sliced

⅓ cup soy sauce

2 tablespoons sake

2 teaspoons sugar

2 teaspoons kosher salt

1 teaspoon neutral-flavored vegetable oil

12 slices Chashu Pork Belly (page 49)

18 ounces Basic Ramen Noodles (page 43 or store-bought) or 12 ounces dried ramen noodles

½ cup Seasoned Bamboo Shoots (page 57)

1 nori sheet, cut into 3-inch ribbons

1. In a large saucepan, heat the sesame oil over medium-high heat until it shimmers. Add the ginger and garlic and cook, stirring, for about 1 minute. Reduce the heat to medium and add the chicken broth and dashi. Bring back to a boil. Reduce the heat to medium-low, stir in the leek, soy sauce, sake, sugar, and salt and let simmer for 6 minutes more.

2. While the broth is heating, heat the vegetable oil in a skillet and warm the pork slices in it for 1 to 2 minutes on each side.

3. Cook the noodles according to the recipe (or package instructions) and then drain well.

4. When the noodles are done cooking, immediately ladle the hot soup, including the slices of leek, into 4 serving bowls. Add ¼ of the noodles to each bowl. Stir gently and lift with chopsticks to coat the noodles. The noodles should float on top somewhat.

5. Top each bowl with 3 slices of pork, ¼ of the Seasoned Bamboo Shoots, and ¼ of the nori. Serve immediately.

Ingredient Tip: *Often, leeks contain lots of sandy grit. To clean them, cut the leek lengthwise and slice it into thin strips. Place in a bowl and cover with water. Agitate the slices, then allow any grit to settle to the bottom. Lift the rinsed leek out, leaving the grit in the bowl.*

ONOMICHI RAMEN

DAIRY-FREE, NUT-FREE

PREP TIME: 15 minutes / **COOK TIME:** 40 minutes

SERVES 4

Onomichi Ramen begins with a clear broth flavored with chicken and pork bones, as well as small dried fish. Onomichi Ramen is served piping hot with a top layer of Rendered Pork Fat, which seals in the heat and coats every mouthful with rich flavor. The toppings are usually hidden under the layer of pork fat and include Chashu Pork Belly, scallions, and sometimes a whole Soy Sauce Egg.

8 cups Pork and Chicken Broth (page 23)

3 ounces niboshi (dried anchovies)

1 tablespoon neutral-flavored vegetable oil

12 slices Chashu Pork Belly (page 49)

18 ounces Basic Ramen Noodles (page 43 or store-bought) or 12 ounces dried ramen noodles

4 Soy Sauce Eggs (page 56)

½ cup Seasoned Bamboo Shoots (page 57)

¼ cup chopped scallions, green and white parts

¼ cup Rendered Pork Fat (page 37), at room temperature

1. In a stockpot, combine the Pork and Chicken Broth and niboshi. Set the pot over medium-high heat and bring to a simmer. Simmer, uncovered, for 40 minutes. Strain the broth through a fine-mesh sieve. Return the strained broth to the stockpot.

2. While the broth is heating, heat the vegetable oil in a skillet and warm the pork slices in it for 1 to 2 minutes on each side.

3. Cook the noodles according to the recipe (or package instructions) and then drain well.

4. When the noodles are done cooking, immediately ladle the hot soup into 4 serving bowls. Add ¼ of the noodles to each bowl. Stir gently and lift with chopsticks to coat the noodles. The noodles should float on top somewhat.

5. Top each bowl with 3 slices of pork, 1 Soy Sauce Egg, ¼ of the Seasoned Bamboo Shoots, and 1 tablespoon of scallions. Spoon the Pork Fat over the top, creating a layer to seal in the heat. Serve immediately.

SPICY TONKOTSU RAMEN WITH GRILLED PORK TENDERLOIN,
PEANUTS, AND CILANTRO, PAGE 85

TONKOTSU RAMEN

Classic Tonkotsu Ramen
with Chashu Pork and
Soy Sauce Eggs 82

Hakata-Style Mountain
of Scallions Ramen 83

Shoyu Tonkotsu with
Chashu Pork, Ginger, and
Kikurage Mushrooms 84

Spicy Tonkotsu Ramen with
Grilled Pork Tenderloin,
Peanuts, and Cilantro 85

Shio Tonkotsu Ramen with
Black Garlic Oil 87

Spicy Miso Tonkotsu Ramen
with Ginger Pork 88

Shoyu Tonkotsu with Shrimp
and Mushrooms 89

Tonkotsu Ramen with Kimchi,
Fried Eggs, and Spam 90

Tantanmen with Minced Pork
and Baby Bok Choy 91

Tonkotsu Ramen with
Mentaiko and Shiitake
Mushrooms 92

Tonkotsu Ramen with Chicken
Chashu, Mushrooms, Corn,
and Black Garlic Oil 93

CLASSIC TONKOTSU RAMEN WITH CHASHU PORK AND SOY SAUCE EGGS

DAIRY-FREE, NUT-FREE

PREP TIME: 15 minutes / **COOK TIME:** 15 minutes

SERVES 4

Tonkotsu ramen is a quintessential comfort food, beginning in this recipe with umami-rich Shio Tare. Tonkotsu, the hearty pork bone broth, gets added before the bowl is filled with tender noodles and topped by melt-in-your-mouth Chashu Pork Belly, egg, pickled ginger, and scallions.

½ cup Shio Tare (page 33)

8 cups Tonkotsu (page 21)

1 teaspoon soy sauce

Pinch kosher salt

1 tablespoon neutral-flavored vegetable oil

12 slices Chashu Pork Belly (page 49)

18 ounces Basic Ramen Noodles (page 43 or store-bought) or 12 ounces dried ramen noodles

2 Soy Sauce Eggs (page 56) or Soft-Boiled Eggs (page 55), sliced in half lengthwise

¼ cup sliced scallions, green and white parts

2 tablespoons Black Garlic Oil (page 38)

¼ cup Red Pickled Ginger (page 58)

1. Spoon 2 tablespoons of the tare into each of 4 serving bowls.

2. In a large saucepan, heat the Tonkotsu over high heat until you see bubbles around the edges and it is just about to boil. Stir in the soy sauce and salt.

3. While the broth is heating, heat the vegetable oil in a skillet and warm the pork slices in it for 1 to 2 minutes on each side.

4. Cook the noodles according to the recipe (or package instructions) and then drain well.

5. When the noodles are finished cooking, immediately ladle the hot broth into the serving bowls over the tare. Add ¼ of the noodles to each bowl. Stir gently and lift with chopsticks to distribute the tare into the broth and to coat the noodles. The noodles should float on top somewhat.

6. Top each bowl with 3 slices of pork, half of 1 egg, 1 tablespoon of scallions, ½ tablespoon of Black Garlic Oil, and 1 tablespoon of Red Pickled Ginger. Serve immediately.

Substitution Tip: *If you don't have any Chashu Pork Belly, you can substitute pulled pork shoulder or ground pork that's been seasoned with soy sauce and browned in a skillet.*

HAKATA-STYLE MOUNTAIN OF SCALLIONS RAMEN

DAIRY-FREE, NUT-FREE

PREP TIME: 15 minutes / **COOK TIME:** 15 minutes

SERVES 4

A specialty in Hakata is *negi yama* ramen, also known as Mountain of Scallions ramen. A typically fatty tonkotsu-based ramen with straight, thicker noodles, it's piled high with sliced scallions. The plentiful piling of fresh scallions provides a bright counterpoint to the Chashu Pork Belly.

½ cup Shio Tare (page 33)

8 cups Tonkotsu (page 21)

1 teaspoon soy sauce

Pinch kosher salt

1 tablespoon neutral-flavored vegetable oil

12 slices Chashu Pork Belly (page 49)

18 ounces Basic Ramen Noodles (page 43 or store-bought) or 12 ounces dried ramen noodles

2 cups sliced scallions, green and white parts

1. Spoon 2 tablespoons of the tare into each of 4 serving bowls.

2. In a large saucepan, heat the Tonkotsu over high heat until you see bubbles around the edges and it is just about to boil. Stir in the soy sauce and salt.

3. While the broth is heating, heat the vegetable oil in a skillet and warm the pork slices in it for 1 to 2 minutes on each side.

4. Cook the noodles according to the recipe (or package instructions) and then drain well.

5. When the noodles are finished cooking, immediately ladle the hot broth into the serving bowls over the tare. Add ¼ of the noodles to each bowl. Stir gently and lift with chopsticks to distribute the tare into the broth and to coat the noodles. The noodles should float on top somewhat.

6. Top each bowl with 3 slices of pork and ½ cup of the scallions. Serve immediately.

SHOYU TONKOTSU WITH CHASHU PORK, GINGER, AND KIKURAGE MUSHROOMS

DAIRY-FREE, NUT-FREE

PREP TIME: 15 minutes / **COOK TIME:** 15 minutes

SERVES 4

Kikurage mushrooms, also known as wood ear mushrooms, are mild in flavor, yet add a pleasingly chewy texture and a luscious mouthfeel. Along with fresh ginger, the mushrooms provide a welcome counterpoint to the fatty, rich Tonkotsu and Chashu Pork Belly.

½ cup Shoyu Tare (page 32)

8 cups Tonkotsu (page 21)

1 teaspoon soy sauce

Pinch kosher salt

1 tablespoon neutral-flavored vegetable oil

12 slices Chashu Pork Belly (page 49)

18 ounces Basic Ramen Noodles (page 43 or store-bought) or 12 ounces dried ramen noodles

4 ounces wood ear mushrooms (if using dried, reconstitute them first), julienned

1 (3-inch) piece of fresh ginger, peeled and cut into thin matchstick pieces

1. Spoon 2 tablespoons of the tare into each of 4 serving bowls.

2. In a large saucepan, heat the Tonkotsu over high heat until you see bubbles around the edges and it is just about to boil. Stir in the soy sauce and salt.

3. While the broth is heating, heat the vegetable oil in a skillet and warm the pork slices in it for 1 to 2 minutes on each side.

4. Cook the noodles according to the recipe (or package instructions) and then drain well.

5. When the noodles are finished cooking, immediately ladle the hot broth into the serving bowls over the tare. Add ¼ of the noodles to each bowl. Stir gently and lift with chopsticks to distribute the tare into the broth and to coat the noodles. The noodles should float on top somewhat.

6. Top each bowl with 3 slices of pork, ¼ of the mushrooms, and ¼ of the ginger. Serve immediately.

SPICY TONKOTSU RAMEN WITH GRILLED PORK TENDERLOIN, PEANUTS, AND CILANTRO

DAIRY-FREE

PREP TIME: 15 minutes, plus 4 hours to marinate / **COOK TIME:** 15 minutes

SERVES 4

Chili peppers aren't that common in Japanese cooking, but they feature prominently in the spice mixture called shichimi togarashi (seven-flavor chili pepper). With its spicy and tart high notes, it pairs well with fatty foods. Here, it flavors pork tenderloin served atop tonkotsu ramen sprinkled with crunchy peanuts and fresh cilantro.

FOR THE PORK

3 tablespoons mirin

2 tablespoons soy sauce

2 tablespoons sesame oil

1 tablespoon shichimi togarashi

1 garlic clove, minced

1 pork tenderloin
  (about 1 pound)

FOR THE RAMEN

½ cup Shoyu Tare (page 32)

8 cups Tonkotsu (page 21)

1 teaspoon soy sauce

Pinch kosher salt

18 ounces Basic Ramen
  Noodles (page 43 or
  store-bought) or 12 ounces
  dried ramen noodles

¼ cup chopped roasted,
  unsalted peanuts

¼ cup chopped cilantro

Shichimi togarashi, for garnish

TO MAKE THE PORK

1. In a medium bowl or resealable plastic bag, combine the mirin, soy sauce, sesame oil, shichimi togarashi, and garlic. Add the pork tenderloin and turn to coat well. Marinate for at least 4 hours, or as long as overnight.

2. Heat a grill or grill pan to medium heat. Grill the pork for 10 to 15 minutes, turning frequently, until the meat is cooked through (145°F on an instant-read meat thermometer).

3. Remove the tenderloin from the grill and let rest for 10 minutes before slicing thinly.

TO MAKE THE RAMEN

1. Spoon 2 tablespoons of the tare into each of 4 serving bowls.

2. In a large saucepan, heat the Tonkotsu over high heat until you see bubbles around the edges and it is just about to boil. Stir in the soy sauce and salt.

3. Cook the noodles according to the recipe (or package instructions) and then drain well.

Continued

4. When the noodles are finished cooking, immediately ladle the hot broth into the serving bowls over the tare. Add ¼ of the noodles to each bowl. Stir gently and lift with chopsticks to distribute the tare into the broth and to coat the noodles. The noodles should float on top somewhat.

5. Top each bowl with 3 slices of the pork, 1 tablespoon of the peanuts, and 1 tablespoon of the cilantro. Top with a sprinkle of shichimi togarashi. Serve immediately.

Ingredient Tip: *Shichimi togarashi is a flavorful blend of seven spices, including dried red chili pepper, dried citrus peel (mandarin orange, tangerine, or yuzu), sesame seeds, and sansho peppercorns. You can find it in Asian markets or the Asian foods aisle of most supermarkets.*

SHIO TONKOTSU RAMEN WITH BLACK GARLIC OIL

DAIRY-FREE, NUT-FREE

PREP TIME: 15 minutes / **COOK TIME:** 15 minutes

SERVES 4

Black Garlic Oil (mayu) is an intense condiment made by cooking fresh garlic in oil until it turns black. On its own, it is extremely bitter, but when you add it to a bowl of ramen, it has a magical effect, bringing earthy complexity and beautifully cutting through the Tonkotsu's inherent fattiness.

½ cup Shio Tare (page 33)

8 cups Tonkotsu (page 21)

1 teaspoon soy sauce

Pinch kosher salt

1 tablespoon neutral-flavored vegetable oil

12 slices Chashu Pork Belly (page 49)

18 ounces Basic Ramen Noodles (page 43 or store-bought) or 12 ounces dried ramen noodles

2 Soy Sauce Eggs (page 56), sliced in half lengthwise

¼ cup sliced scallions, green and white parts

2 tablespoons Black Garlic Oil (page 38)

1. Spoon 2 tablespoons of the tare into each of 4 serving bowls.

2. In a large saucepan, heat the Tonkotsu over high heat until you see bubbles around the edges and it is just about to boil. Stir in the soy sauce and salt.

3. While the broth is heating, heat the vegetable oil in a skillet and warm the pork slices in it for 1 to 2 minutes on each side.

4. Cook the noodles according to the recipe (or package instructions) and then drain well.

5. When the noodles are finished cooking, immediately ladle the hot broth into the serving bowls over the tare. Add ¼ of the noodles to each bowl. Stir gently and lift with chopsticks to distribute the tare into the broth and to coat the noodles. The noodles should float on top somewhat.

6. Top each bowl with 3 slices of pork, half of 1 egg, 1 tablespoon of scallions, and ½ tablespoon of the Black Garlic Oil. Serve immediately.

Substitution Tip: *If you don't have any Soy Sauce Eggs on hand, omit them or substitute Soft-Boiled Eggs (page 55).*

SPICY MISO TONKOTSU RAMEN WITH GINGER PORK

DAIRY-FREE, NUT-FREE

PREP TIME: 15 minutes / **COOK TIME:** 15 minutes

SERVES 4

Spicy Miso Tare and Tonkotsu are flavor powerhouses; combined, they balance each other out. In this tantalizing recipe, the unctuous broth is cut by the spicy tare's heat, and the end result is impossible to resist.

½ cup Spicy Miso Tare (page 31)

8 cups Tonkotsu (page 21)

18 ounces Basic Ramen Noodles (page 43 or store-bought) or 12 ounces dried ramen noodles

Ginger Pork (page 50)

2 Soft-Boiled Eggs (page 55), halved lengthwise

¼ cup sliced scallions, green and white parts

1. Spoon 2 tablespoons of the tare into each of 4 serving bowls.

2. In a large saucepan, heat the Tonkotsu over high heat until you see bubbles around the edges and it is just about to boil.

3. Cook the noodles according to the recipe (or package instructions) and then drain well.

4. When the noodles are done cooking, immediately ladle the hot soup into the serving bowls over the tare. Add ¼ of the noodles to each bowl. Stir gently and lift with chopsticks to distribute the tare into the broth and to coat the noodles. The noodles should float on top somewhat.

5. Top each bowl with ¼ of the Ginger Pork, half of 1 egg, and 1 tablespoon of the scallions. Serve immediately.

SHOYU TONKOTSU WITH SHRIMP AND MUSHROOMS

DAIRY-FREE, NUT-FREE

PREP TIME: 15 minutes / **COOK TIME:** 18 minutes

SERVES 4

A rich Tonkotsu is seasoned with salty Shoyu Tare and spicy chili paste and then topped with plump shrimp and tender mushrooms for a perfectly balanced bowl of ramen. This is a great recipe for any time you are in a rush but want a delicious, nutritious bowl of ramen.

½ cup Shoyu Tare (page 32)

8 cups Tonkotsu (page 21)

½ pound shrimp, peeled and deveined

½ pound button mushrooms, halved

2 tablespoons chili paste (sambal oelek)

2 teaspoons sesame oil

18 ounces Basic Ramen Noodles (page 43 or store-bought) or 12 ounces dried ramen noodles

2 Soft-Boiled Eggs (page 55), halved lengthwise

¼ cup sliced scallions, green and white parts

1 cup bean sprouts

1. Spoon 2 tablespoons of the tare into each of 4 serving bowls.

2. In a large saucepan, heat the Tonkotsu over high heat until you see bubbles around the edges and it is just about to boil. Add the shrimp and mushrooms and continue to simmer for 2 to 3 more minutes, until the shrimp are cooked through. Stir in the chili paste and sesame oil.

3. Cook the noodles according to the recipe (or package instructions) and then drain well.

4. When the noodles are done cooking, immediately ladle the hot broth into the serving bowls over the tare. Leave the shrimp and mushrooms in the pot. Add ¼ of the noodles to each bowl. Stir gently and lift with chopsticks to distribute the tare into the broth and to coat the noodles. The noodles should float on top somewhat.

5. Divide the shrimp and mushrooms among the bowls.

6. Top each bowl with half of 1 egg, 1 tablespoon of scallions, and ¼ cup of bean sprouts.

Substitution Tip: *The shrimp absorbs flavor as it cooks in the broth, but if you have already-cooked shrimp, add them to the bowl along with the other toppings.*

TONKOTSU RAMEN WITH KIMCHI, FRIED EGGS, AND SPAM

DAIRY-FREE, NUT-FREE

PREP TIME: 15 minutes / **COOK TIME:** 20 minutes

SERVES 4

Spam (canned spiced ham) is popular in Asian countries around the world where the United States has had a military presence. In Hawaii, you'll find Spam as musubi (Spam sushi) and as a topping for fried eggs and rice plates. Because it's affordable, shelf-stable, and globally available, it's an obvious way to shake up a bowl of homemade ramen. Just plain crazy or crazy good? You be the judge.

½ cup Shio Tare (page 33)

8 cups Tonkotsu (page 21)

4 (½-inch-thick) slices Spam

1 tablespoon neutral-flavored vegetable oil

4 large eggs

18 ounces Basic Ramen Noodles (page 43 or store-bought) or 12 ounces dried ramen noodles

1 cup kimchi, drained

1. Spoon 2 tablespoons of the tare into each of 4 serving bowls.

2. In a large saucepan, heat the Tonkotsu over high heat until you see bubbles around the edges and it is just about to boil.

3. While the broth is heating, heat a large skillet over medium-high heat. Add the Spam and cook for 2 to 3 minutes, until the bottom of each slice is browned. Flip the Spam slices over and cook until the second side is browned, about 2 minutes more. Remove from the pan.

4. In the same skillet, add the vegetable oil and swirl to coat the pan. Add the eggs and fry to desired doneness, flipping over if desired.

5. Cook the noodles according to the recipe (or package instructions) and then drain well.

6. When the noodles are finished cooking, immediately ladle the hot broth into the serving bowls over the tare. Add ¼ of the noodles to each bowl. Stir gently and lift with chopsticks to distribute the tare into the broth and to coat the noodles. The noodles should float on top somewhat.

7. Top each bowl with a slice of Spam, 1 egg, and ¼ cup of kimchi. Serve immediately.

TANTANMEN WITH MINCED PORK AND BABY BOK CHOY

DAIRY-FREE

PREP TIME: 15 minutes / **COOK TIME:** 20 minutes

Here, Chinese dan dan noodles have been turned into a Japanese ramen dish. In Hiroshima, the most popular version is brothless, but all tantanmen is made to match the Chinese dish's intense spiciness. This recipe calls for Chili Oil (Rayu), while Japanese sesame paste adds nutty flavor.

¼ cup doubanjiang (fermented chili and bean paste)

2 tablespoons Japanese sesame paste

1 teaspoon Sichuan peppercorns, toasted and ground

½ teaspoon ground white pepper

8 cups Tonkotsu (page 21)

8 to 12 baby bok choy heads

1 pound ground pork

3 garlic cloves, minced

2 tablespoons minced fresh ginger

4 scallions, thinly sliced, green and white parts separated

18 ounces Basic Ramen Noodles (page 43 or store-bought) or 12 ounces dried ramen noodles

2 tablespoons Chili Oil (page 39)

2 teaspoons sesame oil

2 tablespoons sesame seeds

1. In a medium bowl, stir together the doubanjiang, sesame paste, Sichuan peppercorns, and white pepper. Set aside.

2. In a large saucepan, heat the Tonkotsu over high heat until it bubbles around the edges and it is just about to boil. Add the baby bok choy and cook for 1 to 2 minutes, until tender. Remove from the broth with a slotted spoon and set aside.

3. Stir half of the doubanjiang mixture into the broth and remove from the heat.

4. Heat a large skillet over medium-high heat. Add the pork and cook, stirring frequently, until browned, about 5 minutes. Add the garlic, ginger, and the whites of the scallions and cook, stirring, for 1 minute. Stir in the remaining doubanjiang mixture and cook, stirring, for 1 minute more. Remove the pan from the heat.

5. Divide the noodles between 4 serving bowls. Ladle the broth on top of the noodles and then top them with ¼ of the bok choy and pork, dividing equally. Garnish with the Chili Oil, sesame oil, scallion greens, and sesame seeds.

Substitution Tip: *If you don't have sesame paste on hand, use a no-sugar-added smooth peanut butter instead.*

TONKOTSU RAMEN WITH MENTAIKO AND SHIITAKE MUSHROOMS

NUT-FREE

PREP TIME: 15 minutes / **COOK TIME:** 20 minutes

Mentaiko is the salted, chile-spiced roe of pollock or cod, and often used as a filling for onigiri (Japanese rice balls). Here, it makes a great topping for a bowl of creamy tonkotsu ramen. The salty roe pairs beautifully with butter, and the addition of rich sautéed mushrooms makes a perfect finishing touch.

½ cup Shio Tare (page 33)

8 cups Tonkotsu (page 21)

2 tablespoons butter

8 ounces shiitake mushrooms, sliced

18 ounces Basic Ramen Noodles (page 43 or store-bought) or 12 ounces dried ramen noodles

¼ cup sliced scallions, green and white parts

1 sheet nori, cut into 3-inch strips

2 ounces mentaiko

1. Spoon 2 tablespoons of the tare into each of 4 serving bowls.

2. In a large saucepan, heat the Tonkotsu over high heat until it bubbles around the edges and it is just about to boil.

3. While the broth is heating, melt the butter in a large skillet over medium-high heat. Add the mushrooms and cook, stirring occasionally, until softened and beginning to brown, about 5 minutes. Remove the pan from the heat.

4. Cook the noodles according to the recipe (or package instructions) and then drain well.

5. When the noodles are finished cooking, immediately ladle the hot broth into the serving bowls over the tare. Add ¼ of the noodles to each bowl. Stir gently and lift with chopsticks to distribute the tare into the broth and to coat the noodles. The noodles should float on top somewhat.

6. Top each bowl with ¼ of the mushrooms, 1 tablespoon of the scallions, several strips of nori, and a heaping spoonful of mentaiko.

Substitution Tip: *If you can't find mentaiko, substitute spicy tobiko (flying fish roe) or ikura (salmon roe), both also available at Asian markets.*

TONKOTSU RAMEN WITH CHICKEN CHASHU, MUSHROOMS, CORN, AND BLACK GARLIC OIL

NUT-FREE

PREP TIME: 15 minutes / **COOK TIME:** 20 minutes

Like Chashu Pork Belly, slices of Chicken Chashu make a filling topping for a bowl of ramen. The chicken here is highlighted by the fresh mushrooms and corn. A dash of Black Garlic Oil balances out the sweetness of the corn with a hint of bitterness.

½ cup Shio Tare (page 33)

8 cups Tonkotsu (page 21)

2 tablespoons butter

8 ounces shiitake mushrooms, sliced

½ cup corn kernels (from 1 ear of corn)

12 slices Chicken Chashu (page 53)

18 ounces Basic Ramen Noodles (page 43 or store-bought) or 12 ounces dried ramen noodles

4 teaspoons Black Garlic Oil (page 38)

1. Spoon 2 tablespoons of the tare into each of 4 serving bowls.

2. In a large saucepan, heat the Tonkotsu over high heat until you see bubbles around the edges and it is just about to boil.

3. While the broth is heating, melt the butter in a large skillet over medium-high heat. Add the mushrooms and cook, stirring occasionally, until softened and beginning to brown, about 5 minutes. Remove the mushrooms from the pan.

4. Add the corn to the same skillet and cook just until heated through and beginning to brown, about 3 minutes. Remove the corn from the pan.

5. In the same skillet, heat the chicken for 1 to 2 minutes per side over medium heat.

6. Cook the noodles according to the recipe (or package instructions) and then drain well.

7. When the noodles are finished cooking, immediately ladle the hot broth into the serving bowls over the tare. Add ¼ of the noodles to each bowl. Stir gently and lift with chopsticks to distribute the tare into the broth and to coat the noodles. The noodles should float on top somewhat.

8. Top each bowl with ¼ of the mushrooms, ¼ of the corn, 3 slices of chicken, and 1 teaspoon of Black Garlic Oil. Serve immediately.

SHOYU RAMEN WITH LITTLENECK CLAMS,
SCALLIONS, AND BUTTER, PAGE 116

SHOYU RAMEN

Shoyu Ramen with Ginger-Braised Pork and Kimchi 96

Shoyu Ramen with Seared Steak, Scallions, and Sesame Oil 98

Shoyu Ramen with Chicken Katsu, Broccoli Rabe, and Scallions 100

Shoyu Ramen with Pork Katsu, Spinach, and Chili Oil 102

Shoyu Ramen with Shrimp-and-Pork Wontons and Baby Bok Choy 103

Shoyu Ramen with Spicy Ground Lamb, Spinach, and Scallions 105

Creamy Paitan Shoyu Ramen with Ginger Pork and Tender Greens 106

Creamy Paitan Shoyu Ramen with Soft-Shell Crab and Tender Greens 107

Vegan Shoyu Ramen with Shiitake Mushrooms, Nori, and Scallion Oil 109

Shoyu Wild Mushroom Ramen with Meyer Lemon and Kabocha Squash 110

Spicy Shoyu Ramen with Corn, Silken Tofu, and Bean Sprouts 112

Asahikawa Double Broth Ramen with Scallops, Mushrooms, and Scallion Oil 113

Cheesy Ramen with Chili Oil, Soy Sauce Eggs, and Corn 114

Shoyu Ramen with Chicken Livers and Garlic Chives 115

Shoyu Ramen with Littleneck Clams, Scallions, and Butter 116

SHOYU RAMEN WITH GINGER-BRAISED PORK AND KIMCHI

DAIRY-FREE, NUT-FREE

PREP TIME: 15 minutes / **COOK TIME:** 3 hours, plus 15 minutes

SERVES 4

The inclusion of ginger-braised pork elevates this ramen. Although the succulent pork takes a while to cook, the actual preparation couldn't be easier. When the broth, tare, chicken fat, noodles, and Soft-Boiled Eggs are already made, this delicious ramen requires little additional work.

FOR THE PORK

1 tablespoon sesame oil

1 (3-inch) piece fresh ginger, sliced into thick rounds

2 pounds pork shoulder, cut into large cubes

5 tablespoons white miso

3 tablespoons shoyu or low-sodium soy sauce

½ cup mirin

1 cup water

FOR THE RAMEN

½ cup Shoyu Tare (page 32)

¼ cup Rendered Chicken Fat (page 36)

8 cups Clear Chicken Broth (page 17)

18 ounces Basic Ramen Noodles (page 43 or store-bought) or 12 ounces dried ramen noodles

2 Soft-Boiled Eggs (page 55), sliced in half lengthwise

1 cup kimchi, drained

¼ cup sliced scallions, green and white parts

TO MAKE THE PORK

1. In a large saucepan, heat the sesame oil over medium heat for about 1 minute. Add the ginger and cook, stirring frequently, until the ginger is golden brown, about 1 minute. Add the pork and cook, stirring occasionally, until it is lightly browned on all sides, about 8 minutes.

2. In a mixing bowl, stir together the miso, shoyu, mirin, and water and combine well.

3. Pour the miso mixture over the pork in the saucepan. Raise the heat to medium-high and bring to a boil. Reduce the heat to low, cover, and simmer for about 3 hours, or until the pork is fork-tender. Transfer the pork from the braising liquid to a bowl and shred with 2 forks. Return the shredded meat to the braising liquid.

TO MAKE THE RAMEN

1. Spoon 2 tablespoons of the tare and 1 tablespoon of the chicken fat into each of 4 serving bowls.

2. In a large saucepan, heat the Clear Chicken Broth over high heat until it is just about to boil.

3. Cook the noodles according to the recipe (or package instructions) and then drain well.

4. When the noodles are done cooking, immediately ladle the hot soup into the serving bowls over the tare and fat. Add ¼ of the noodles to each bowl. Stir gently and lift with chopsticks to distribute the tare into the broth and to coat the noodles. The noodles should float on top somewhat.

5. Top each bowl with about ¼ cup of shredded pork, half of 1 egg, ¼ cup of the kimchi, and 1 tablespoon of the scallions. Serve immediately.

Repurposing Tip: *Ginger-Braised Pork is also delicious served over steamed rice with a side of roasted vegetables.*

SHOYU RAMEN WITH SEARED STEAK, SCALLIONS, AND SESAME OIL

DAIRY-FREE, NUT-FREE

PREP TIME: 15 minutes, plus 30 minutes to marinate / **COOK TIME:** 25 minutes

SERVES 4

Soy-marinated steak makes a sublime topping for a shoyu ramen. Seared to a perfect medium-rare and cut into strips, the meat is tender, juicy, and beautifully caramelized on the outside. A sprinkling of scallions and float of nutty sesame oil are all the finishing touches you need.

FOR THE STEAK

2 tablespoons soy sauce

2 tablespoons sake

1 tablespoon sugar

1 (½-pound) New York strip steak

Pinch salt

Freshly ground black pepper

1 tablespoon neutral-flavored vegetable oil

1 garlic clove, thinly sliced

FOR THE RAMEN

½ cup Shoyu Tare (page 32)

8 cups Clear Chicken Broth (page 17)

18 ounces Basic Ramen Noodles (page 43 or store-bought) or 12 ounces dried ramen noodles

¼ cup sliced scallions, green and white parts

2 tablespoons sesame oil

TO MAKE THE STEAK

1. In a medium bowl, stir together the soy sauce, sake, and sugar.

2. Season the steak with salt and pepper. Add the steak to the sauce and turn to coat. Marinate the steak for at least 30 minutes, or in the refrigerator for as long as overnight.

3. In a large skillet, heat the vegetable oil over medium-high heat until it shimmers. Add the garlic and cook, stirring, just until it begins to brown, about 1 minute.

4. Add the steak to the skillet and cook, turning once, to desired doneness, about 3 minutes per side for medium-rare. Pour the marinade mixture over the steak and turn the meat to coat. Remove the meat from the pan and set aside to rest for at least 10 minutes. Slice across the grain into ⅛-inch-thick slices.

TO MAKE THE RAMEN

1. Spoon 2 tablespoons of the tare into each of 4 serving bowls.

2. In a large saucepan, heat the Clear Chicken Broth over high heat until it is just about to boil.

3. Cook the noodles according to the recipe (or package instructions) and then drain well.

4. When the noodles are done cooking, immediately ladle the hot soup into the serving bowls over the tare. Add ¼ of the noodles to each bowl. Stir gently and lift with chopsticks to distribute the tare into the broth and to coat the noodles. The noodles should float on top somewhat.

5. Top each bowl with about ¼ of the steak, 1 tablespoon of scallions, and 1½ teaspoons of sesame oil. Serve immediately.

Substitution Tip: *Tender, flavorful New York strip steak makes a great topping for ramen, but you can substitute other cuts like rib eye and flat iron.*

SHOYU RAMEN WITH CHICKEN KATSU, BROCCOLI RABE, AND SCALLIONS

DAIRY-FREE, NUT-FREE

PREP TIME: 20 minutes / **COOK TIME:** 25 minutes

SERVES 4

This ramen is a textural treat: a Clear Chicken Broth topped with crispy chicken. *Katsu* is a breaded meat cutlet (pork, chicken, or beef) that's been pounded thin, breaded, and deep-fried. Make your own katsu sauce by combining ketchup, Worcestershire, and soy, or find it bottled at an Asian market or in your supermarket's Asian foods aisle.

FOR THE CHICKEN

1 large boneless, skin-
  less chicken breast
  (about 1 pound)
¾ teaspoon salt
¼ teaspoon freshly ground
  black pepper
Neutral-flavored vegetable oil,
  for deep-frying
1 large egg, lightly beaten
1 cup panko bread crumbs

FOR THE RAMEN

½ cup Shoyu Tare (page 32)
8 cups Clear Chicken Broth
  (page 17)
¾ pound broccoli rabe
18 ounces Basic Ramen
  Noodles (page 43 or
  store-bought) or 12 ounces
  dried ramen noodles
¼ cup sliced scallions, green
  and white parts
¼ cup katsu sauce

TO MAKE THE CHICKEN

1. Slice the chicken breast horizontally into two thin slices. Cut each slice into 2 equal-size pieces. Season them with the salt and pepper and set aside.

2. Fill a deep pot with about 3 inches of vegetable oil over high heat until it shimmers.

3. Put the egg and bread crumbs in separate wide, shallow bowls. Dip a chicken piece first into the egg and then into the bread crumbs, turning to coat well. Dip the coated chicken into the egg a second time, and then coat with the bread crumbs again. Repeat with all the chicken pieces.

4. Gently lower each piece of chicken into the hot oil and cook, turning once, for about 4 minutes, until golden brown on both sides. Transfer the cooked chicken pieces to a paper towel–lined plate. Let the chicken cool for at least 5 minutes and then cut each piece into strips.

TO MAKE THE RAMEN

1. Spoon 2 tablespoons of the tare into each of 4 serving bowls.

2. In a large saucepan, heat the Clear Chicken Broth over high heat until it is just about to boil. Add the broccoli rabe and simmer for 4 minutes, or until crisp-tender. Using a slotted spoon, remove from the broth.

3. Cook the noodles according to the recipe (or package instructions) and then drain well.

4. When the noodles are done cooking, immediately ladle the hot soup into the serving bowls over the tare. Add ¼ of the noodles to each bowl. Stir gently and lift with chopsticks to distribute the tare into the broth and to coat the noodles. The noodles should float on top somewhat.

5. Top each bowl with about 1 tablespoon of the scallions and ¼ of the broccoli rabe. Place 1 chicken piece on top and drizzle the katsu sauce over the chicken. Serve immediately.

Ingredient Tip: *Broccoli rabe looks a lot like unruly broccoli, but it's related to turnips. If you can't find broccoli rabe, substitute broccoli and cook it the same way (although it may need a minute longer to become crisp-tender).*

SHOYU RAMEN WITH PORK KATSU, SPINACH, AND CHILI OIL

DAIRY-FREE, NUT-FREE

PREP TIME: 20 minutes / **COOK TIME:** 25 minutes

SERVES 4

Crispy Pork Katsu strips make this ramen a showstopper. With Seasoned Bamboo Shoots, spinach, and a dash of Chili Oil, you have a deliciously well-rounded meal.

½ cup Shoyu Tare (page 32)

8 cups Clear Chicken Broth (page 17)

4 cups fresh spinach

18 ounces Basic Ramen Noodles (page 43 or store-bought) or 12 ounces dried ramen noodles

½ cup Seasoned Bamboo Shoots (page 57)

¼ cup sliced scallions, green and white parts

4 teaspoons Chili Oil (page 39) or bottled chili oil

12 strips Pork Katsu (page 52)

¼ cup katsu sauce

1. Spoon 2 tablespoons of the tare into each of 4 serving bowls.

2. In a large saucepan, heat the Clear Chicken Broth over high heat until it is just about to boil. Add the spinach to the broth and cook for 1 to 2 minutes, until just wilted. Remove the spinach from the broth using a slotted spoon or tongs and set aside.

3. Cook the noodles according to the recipe (or package instructions) and then drain well.

4. When the noodles are done cooking, immediately ladle the hot soup into the serving bowls over the tare. Add ¼ of the noodles to each bowl. Stir gently and lift with chopsticks to distribute the tare into the broth and to coat the noodles. The noodles should float on top somewhat.

5. Top each bowl with ¼ of the wilted spinach, ¼ of the Seasoned Bamboo Shoots, ¼ of the scallions, and 1 teaspoon of the Chili Oil. Place 3 pork pieces on top and drizzle the katsu sauce over the pork. Serve immediately.

Substitution Tip: *See the recipe for Shoyu Ramen with Chicken Katsu, Broccoli Rabe, and Scallions (page 100) for instructions for making this dish with chicken instead of pork.*

SHOYU RAMEN WITH SHRIMP-AND-PORK WONTONS AND BABY BOK CHOY

DAIRY-FREE, NUT-FREE

PREP TIME: 20 minutes / **COOK TIME:** 20 minutes

SERVES 4

Noodles are great, but wontons—noodle wrappers filled with seasoned meat and shellfish—are equally amazing. This ramen gives you both—a shoyu-based soup full of tender noodles, topped by plump shrimp-and-pork wontons.

FOR THE WONTONS

¼ pound peeled and deveined shrimp, chopped

¼ pound ground pork

1 teaspoon sesame oil

¼ teaspoon salt

1 teaspoon cornstarch

20 wonton wrappers

FOR THE RAMEN

½ cup Shoyu Tare (page 32)

8 cups Clear Chicken Broth (page 17)

⅓ pound baby bok choy

18 ounces Basic Ramen Noodles (page 43 or store-bought) or 12 ounces dried ramen noodles

¼ cup sliced scallions, green and white parts

4 teaspoons Chili Oil (page 39) or bottled chili oil

TO MAKE THE WONTONS

1. In a medium bowl, combine the shrimp, pork, sesame oil, salt, and cornstarch and mix well.

2. Lay a wonton wrapper on your work surface and place about 1 teaspoon of the shrimp and pork mixture in the center. Dip your finger in a small bowl of water and wet the corners of the wrapper to help it seal, then pinch the wrapper together to seal in the filling. Repeat with the remaining filling and wrappers. Set aside.

TO MAKE THE RAMEN

1. Spoon 2 tablespoons of the tare into each of 4 serving bowls.

2. In a large saucepan, heat the Clear Chicken Broth over high heat until it is just about to boil. Add the wontons to the pot. Once they float, about 2 to 3 minutes, scoop them out with a slotted spoon and set aside.

3. Add the bok choy to the broth and then remove the broth from the heat.

4. Cook the noodles according to the recipe (or package instructions) and then drain well.

Continued

5. When the noodles are done cooking, immediately ladle the hot soup into the serving bowls over the tare. Leave the bok choy in the pot. Add ¼ of the noodles to each bowl. Stir gently and lift with chopsticks to distribute the tare into the broth and to coat the noodles. The noodles should float on top somewhat.

6. Top each bowl with 5 wontons, ¼ of the bok choy, 1 tablespoon of the scallions, and 1 teaspoon of Chili Oil. Serve immediately.

Substitution Tip: *To save time, you can find high-quality frozen wontons in most Asian markets' freezer sections. Cook them from frozen as in step 2. They will just take a little longer to float (about 3 to 5 minutes).*

SHOYU RAMEN WITH SPICY GROUND LAMB, SPINACH, AND SCALLIONS

DAIRY-FREE, NUT-FREE

PREP TIME: 10 minutes / **COOK TIME:** 20 minutes

SERVES 4

As a rich, intensely flavored meat, lamb works nicely atop a lighter chicken broth–based ramen. Wilted spinach and fresh scallions bring contrast, making this a balanced bowl.

FOR THE LAMB

1 pound ground lamb

½ teaspoon salt

1 garlic clove, minced

1 (1-inch) piece fresh ginger, peeled and minced

1 teaspoon red pepper flakes

1 teaspoon soy sauce

FOR THE RAMEN

½ cup Shoyu Tare (page 32)

8 cups Clear Chicken Broth (page 17)

⅓ pound fresh spinach

18 ounces Basic Ramen Noodles (page 43 or store-bought) or 12 ounces dried ramen noodles

¼ cup sliced scallions, green and white parts

TO MAKE THE LAMB

Heat a large skillet over medium-high heat. Add the lamb and salt and cook, stirring occasionally and breaking up with a spatula, until the meat is browned, about 5 minutes. Add the garlic, ginger, and red pepper flakes and cook, stirring, for 1 minute more. Stir in the soy sauce and remove from the heat.

TO MAKE THE RAMEN

1. Spoon 2 tablespoons of the tare into each of 4 serving bowls.

2. In a large saucepan, heat the Clear Chicken Broth over high heat until it is just about to boil. Add the spinach to the broth and cook for 1 to 2 minutes, until just wilted. Remove the spinach from the broth using a slotted spoon or tongs and set aside.

3. Cook the noodles according to the recipe (or package instructions) and then drain well.

4. When the noodles are done cooking, immediately ladle the hot soup into the serving bowls over the tare. Add ¼ of the noodles to each bowl. Stir gently and lift with chopsticks to distribute the tare into the broth and to coat the noodles. The noodles should float on top somewhat.

5. Top each bowl with ¼ of the wilted spinach, 1 tablespoon of scallions, and ¼ of the lamb mixture. Serve immediately.

Substitution Tip: *Ginger Pork (page 50) also works well in this recipe; for added zing, drizzle with a teaspoon of Chili Oil (page 39).*

CREAMY PAITAN SHOYU RAMEN WITH GINGER PORK AND TENDER GREENS

DAIRY-FREE, NUT-FREE

PREP TIME: 10 minutes / **COOK TIME:** 20 minutes

SERVES 4

This is the bowl of ramen I want when I'm feeling under the weather. With its creamy, thick broth, flavorful pork, and sweet greens, it is a nourishing bowl of comfort.

½ cup Shoyu Tare (page 32)

8 cups "Creamy" Chicken Broth (page 19)

4 cups fresh spinach

18 ounces Basic Ramen Noodles (page 43 or store-bought) or 12 ounces dried ramen noodles

Ginger Pork (page 50)

2 Soft-Boiled Eggs (page 55), halved lengthwise

1. Spoon 2 tablespoons of the tare into each of 4 serving bowls.

2. In a large saucepan, heat the "Creamy" Chicken Broth over high heat until it is just about to boil. Add the spinach to the broth and cook for 1 to 2 minutes, until just wilted. Remove the spinach from the broth using a slotted spoon or tongs and set aside.

3. Cook the noodles according to the recipe (or package instructions) and then drain well.

4. When the noodles are done cooking, immediately ladle the hot soup into the serving bowls over the tare. Add ¼ of the noodles to each bowl. Stir gently and lift with chopsticks to distribute the tare into the broth and to coat the noodles. The noodles should float on top somewhat.

5. Top each bowl with ¼ of the wilted spinach, ¼ of the Ginger Pork, and half of 1 egg. Serve immediately.

Substitution Tip: *Spinach can be quickly wilted in the hot broth, but you can also quickly sauté other greens like Swiss chard, kale, or mustard greens to add even more texture.*

CREAMY PAITAN SHOYU RAMEN WITH SOFT-SHELL CRAB AND TENDER GREENS

DAIRY-FREE, NUT-FREE

PREP TIME: 10 minutes / **COOK TIME:** 20 minutes

SERVES 4

This decadent ramen starts with "Creamy" Chicken Broth and is topped with a tempura-style fried soft-shell crab. As the name implies, these crabs have completely edible soft shells. A seasonal treat, soft-shell crabs are only available from late spring to early summer.

FOR THE SOFT-SHELL CRABS

¾ cup all-purpose flour

2 teaspoons baking powder

1 cup cold club soda or seltzer water

Vegetable oil for frying the crabs

4 soft-shell crabs

FOR THE RAMEN

½ cup Shoyu Tare (page 32)

8 cups "Creamy" Chicken Broth (page 19)

4 cups fresh spinach

18 ounces Basic Ramen Noodles (page 43 or store-bought) or 12 ounces dried ramen noodles

¼ cup sliced scallions, green and white parts

TO MAKE THE SOFT-SHELL CRABS

1. In a medium bowl, whisk together the flour, baking powder, and club soda to make a batter.

2. In a heavy skillet, heat ¼ inch of vegetable oil over medium-high heat until it shimmers.

3. Dunk a crab in the batter to coat, letting the excess drip off into the bowl, and then carefully place it in the oil and fry for 1 to 2 minutes on each side until golden brown and crisp. Transfer the cooked crab to a paper towel–lined plate to drain. Repeat with the remaining crabs.

TO MAKE THE RAMEN

1. Spoon 2 tablespoons of the tare into each of 4 serving bowls.

2. In a large saucepan, heat the "Creamy" Chicken Broth over high heat until it is just about to boil. Add the spinach to the broth and cook for 1 to 2 minutes, until just wilted. Remove the spinach from the broth using a slotted spoon or tongs and set aside.

3. Cook the noodles according to the recipe (or package instructions) and then drain well.

Continued

4. When the noodles are done cooking, immediately ladle the hot soup into the serving bowls over the tare. Add ¼ of the noodles to each bowl. Stir gently and lift with chopsticks to distribute the tare into the broth and to coat the noodles. The noodles should float on top somewhat.

5. Top each bowl with 1 fried crab, ¼ of the wilted spinach, and 1 tablespoon of scallions. Serve immediately.

Substitution Tip: *If you can't get your hands on any soft-shell crab, substitute large prawns. Dip them (peeled, but with their tails left on) in the tempura batter and fry.*

VEGAN SHOYU RAMEN WITH SHIITAKE MUSHROOMS, NORI, AND SCALLION OIL

DAIRY-FREE, NUT-FREE, VEGAN

PREP TIME: 10 minutes / **COOK TIME:** 20 minutes

SERVES 4

This simple vegan ramen is loaded with umami thanks to the base of Shiitake Dashi and the added shiitake mushrooms sautéed with garlic. Aromatic Scallion Oil adds another flavorful layer with its gentle notes.

1 tablespoon neutral-flavored vegetable oil

4 ounces fresh shiitake mushrooms, sliced

1 garlic clove, minced

Pinch salt

½ cup Shoyu Tare (page 32)

8 cups Shiitake Dashi (page 26)

18 ounces Basic Ramen Noodles (page 43 or store-bought) or 12 ounces dried ramen noodles

1 sheet nori, cut into 3-inch strips

¼ cup sliced scallions, green and white parts

4 teaspoons Scallion Oil (page 40)

1. In a large skillet, heat the vegetable oil over medium-high heat until it shimmers. Add the mushrooms, garlic, and salt and cook, stirring occasionally, until the mushrooms are softened, about 5 minutes.

2. Spoon 2 tablespoons of the tare into each of 4 serving bowls.

3. In a large saucepan, heat the Shiitake Dashi over high heat until it is just about to boil.

4. Cook the noodles according to the recipe (or package instructions) and then drain well.

5. When the noodles are done cooking, immediately ladle the hot soup into the serving bowls over the tare. Add ¼ of the noodles to each bowl. Stir gently and lift with chopsticks to distribute the tare into the broth and to coat the noodles. The noodles should float on top somewhat.

6. Top each bowl with ¼ of the mushrooms, ¼ of the nori, and 1 tablespoon of scallions. Drizzle 1 teaspoon of the Scallion Oil over each serving. Serve immediately.

Repurposing Tip: You can use reconstituted dried shiitake mushrooms in place of fresh ones. If you have mushrooms left over from making the Shiitake Dashi, use them!

SHOYU WILD MUSHROOM RAMEN WITH MEYER LEMON AND KABOCHA SQUASH

DAIRY-FREE, NUT-FREE, VEGAN

PREP TIME: 10 minutes / **COOK TIME:** 25 minutes

SERVES 4

Loaded with flavorful ingredients, this exotic ramen starts with an umami-rich Shiitake Dashi; Shoyu Tare adds more umami; and the juice of a charred Meyer lemon lends acidity and smokiness. The addition of sautéed matsutake mushrooms and Roasted Kabocha Squash make it a filling soup. If you can't find matsutakes, you can substitute trumpets or a similarly textured mushroom.

1 Meyer lemon, halved

2 tablespoons neutral-flavored vegetable oil

8 ounces fresh matsutake mushrooms, sliced

Pinch salt

½ cup Shoyu Tare (page 32)

8 cups Shiitake Dashi (page 26)

18 ounces Basic Ramen Noodles (page 43 or store-bought) or 12 ounces dried ramen noodles

Roasted Kabocha Squash (page 60)

¼ cup sliced scallions, green and white parts

1. Heat a heavy skillet over high heat until it is nearly smoking. Add the lemon halves, cut side down, and cook until they are charred, about 8 minutes. Remove from the heat and let cool. Juice the lemons and strain the juice through a fine-mesh sieve.

2. In a large skillet, heat the vegetable oil over medium-high heat until it shimmers. Add the mushrooms and salt and cook, stirring occasionally, until the mushrooms are softened, about 5 minutes.

3. Spoon 2 tablespoons of the tare and ½ teaspoon of the lemon juice into each of 4 serving bowls.

4. In a large saucepan, heat the Shiitake Dashi over high heat until it is just about to boil.

5. Cook the noodles according to the recipe (or package instructions) and then drain well.

6. When the noodles are done cooking, immediately ladle the hot soup into the serving bowls over the tare and lemon juice. Add ¼ of the noodles to each bowl. Stir gently and lift with chopsticks to distribute the tare and lemon juice into the broth and to coat the noodles. The noodles should float on top somewhat.

7. Top each bowl with ¼ of the mushrooms, ¼ of the kabocha squash, and 1 tablespoon of the scallions. Serve immediately.

Repurposing Tip: *Save the matsutake mushroom trimmings and use them to make mushroom dashi. You'll need about 2 cups' worth, but they keep well in a bag in the freezer.*

SPICY SHOYU RAMEN WITH CORN, SILKEN TOFU, AND BEAN SPROUTS

DAIRY-FREE, NUT-FREE

PREP TIME: 10 minutes / **COOK TIME:** 25 minutes

SERVES 4

This light ramen starts with an Awase Dashi and Shoyu Tare. Sweet corn kernels, luscious silken tofu, and crunchy bean sprouts give it fresh flavor and lots of contrasting texture.

½ cup Shoyu Tare (page 32)

8 cups Awase Dashi (page 25)

18 ounces Basic Ramen Noodles (page 43 or store-bought) or 12 ounces dried ramen noodles

1 cup fresh corn kernels (from 2 ears of corn)

6 ounces silken tofu, diced

½ cup bean sprouts

¼ cup sliced scallions, green and white parts

4 teaspoons Chili Oil (page 39)

1. Spoon 2 tablespoons of the tare into each of 4 serving bowls.

2. In a large saucepan, heat the Awase Dashi over high heat until it is just about to boil.

3. Cook the noodles according to the recipe (or package instructions) and then drain well.

4. When the noodles are done cooking, immediately ladle the hot soup into the serving bowls over the tare. Add ¼ of the noodles to each bowl. Stir gently and lift with chopsticks to distribute the tare into the broth and to coat the noodles. The noodles should float on top somewhat.

5. Top each bowl with ¼ cup of the corn, ¼ of the tofu, 2 tablespoons of bean sprouts, and 1 tablespoon of the scallions. Drizzle 1 teaspoon of Chili Oil over each serving. Serve immediately.

ASAHIKAWA DOUBLE BROTH RAMEN WITH SCALLOPS, MUSHROOMS, AND SCALLION OIL

DAIRY-FREE, NUT-FREE

PREP TIME: 10 minutes / **COOK TIME:** 20 minutes

SERVES 4

Asahikawa is located in Hokkaido's inland area, but has historically been a hub for seafood being transported across the island. Like other Asahikawa-style ramens, this starts with a "double broth"—a mixture of Tonkotsu and Awase Dashi.

4 dried wood ear mushrooms

2 tablespoons butter

12 fresh sea scallops, patted dry

Salt, for seasoning

½ cup Shoyu Tare (page 32)

6 cups Tonkotsu (page 21)

2 cups Awase Dashi (page 25)

18 ounces Basic Ramen Noodles (page 43 or store-bought) or 12 ounces dried ramen noodles

¼ cup sliced scallions, green and white parts

4 teaspoons Scallion Oil (page 40)

1. Place the wood ear mushrooms in a small bowl and cover with boiling water. Let the mushrooms sit for about 10 minutes, and then drain them and cut them into strips.

2. In a large, heavy skillet, melt the butter over medium-high heat until it bubbles. Season the scallops with salt and add them to the skillet. Cook for about 2 minutes per side, until the scallops are golden brown and just barely cooked through. Set aside.

3. Spoon 2 tablespoons of the tare into each of 4 serving bowls.

4. In a large saucepan, heat the Tonkotsu and Awase Dashi over high heat until it is just about to boil.

5. Cook the noodles according to the recipe (or package instructions) and then drain well. When the noodles are done cooking, immediately ladle the hot soup into the serving bowls over the tare. Add ¼ of the noodles to each bowl. Stir gently and lift with chopsticks to distribute the tare into the broth and to coat the noodles. The noodles should float on top somewhat.

6. Top each bowl with 1 mushrooms, 3 scallops, and 1 tablespoon of the scallions. Drizzle 1 teaspoon of Scallion Oil over each serving. Serve immediately.

Ingredient Tip: *Sea scallops, also called day-boat or diver scallops, are caught in the ocean as opposed to protected bays. Usually 1½ to 2 inches across, they are much larger than bay scallops.*

CHEESY RAMEN WITH CHILI OIL, SOY SAUCE EGGS, AND CORN

NUT-FREE

PREP TIME: 10 minutes / **COOK TIME:** 15 minutes

SERVES 4

Cheese on ramen may sound incongruous, but it is most definitely "a thing" popularized in America by the celebrity chef Roy Choi. Some ramen-yas use a dry, hard cheese, while others go full "dorm food" with American cheese. Here, a nutty, aged Gouda stands up well to the Tonkotsu.

½ cup Shoyu Tare (page 32)

8 cups Tonkotsu (page 21)

18 ounces Basic Ramen Noodles (page 43 or store-bought) or 12 ounces dried ramen noodles

1 cup grated aged Gouda cheese

2 Soy Sauce Eggs (page 56), halved

1 cup fresh corn kernels (from 2 ears of corn)

¼ cup sliced scallions, green and white parts

4 teaspoons Chili Oil (page 39)

1. Spoon 2 tablespoons of the tare into each of 4 serving bowls.

2. In a large saucepan, heat the Tonkotsu over high heat until it is just about to boil.

3. Cook the noodles according to the recipe (or package instructions) and then drain well.

4. When the noodles are done cooking, immediately ladle the hot soup into the serving bowls over the tare. Add ¼ of the noodles to each bowl. Stir gently and lift with chopsticks to distribute the tare into the broth and to coat the noodles. The noodles should float on top somewhat.

5. Top each bowl with ¼ cup of cheese, half of 1 egg, ¼ cup of the corn, and 1 tablespoon of the scallions. Drizzle 1 teaspoon of Chili Oil over each serving. Serve immediately.

SHOYU RAMEN WITH CHICKEN LIVERS AND GARLIC CHIVES

NUT-FREE

PREP TIME: 20 minutes / **COOK TIME:** 15 minutes

SERVES 4

Japanese chefs strive to use every part of the animal and no-waste cooking is a point of pride. As a result, the tasty bits that often get discarded are showcased in Japanese cuisine. Pan-seared chicken livers, used here as a delightful topping, is a perfect example.

8 or 12 small chicken livers

2 tablespoons soy sauce

2 tablespoons mirin

2 tablespoons butter

½ cup Shoyu Tare (page 32)

8 cups "Creamy" Chicken Broth (page 19)

18 ounces Basic Ramen Noodles (page 43 or store-bought) or 12 ounces dried ramen noodles

¼ cup sliced garlic chives

1. Place the chicken livers in a bowl and cover with cold water. Let stand for about 10 minutes, and then drain. Pat the livers dry with paper towels. Return the livers to the dry bowl and add the soy sauce and mirin. Let marinate for 10 minutes more.

2. In a heavy skillet, melt the butter over medium-high heat. When the butter is bubbling, add the chicken livers and cook, turning once, until well-browned, about 4 minutes per side. Transfer to a paper towel–lined plate.

3. Spoon 2 tablespoons of the tare into each of 4 serving bowls.

4. In a large saucepan, heat the "Creamy" Chicken Broth over high heat until it is just about to boil.

5. Cook the noodles according to the recipe (or package instructions) and then drain well.

6. When the noodles are done cooking, immediately ladle the hot soup into the serving bowls over the tare. Add ¼ of the noodles to each bowl. Stir gently and lift with chopsticks to distribute the tare into the broth and to coat the noodles. The noodles should float on top somewhat.

7. Top each bowl with 2 or 3 chicken livers and 1 tablespoon of the garlic chives. Serve immediately.

Ingredient Tip: *Garlic chives are similar to onion chives, yet have a delicate but distinct garlic flavor. If you can't find them, substitute regular chives.*

SHOYU RAMEN WITH LITTLENECK CLAMS, SCALLIONS, AND BUTTER

NUT-FREE

PREP TIME: 10 minutes / **COOK TIME:** 25 minutes

SERVES 4

Seafood is abundant in Japan, so it's not surprising that it is featured in many ramens. Clams are easy to cook, inexpensive, and make an impressive visual statement atop a bowl of ramen tinged with butter.

1 pound live littleneck clams, scrubbed clean

½ cup Shoyu Tare (page 32)

8 cups "Creamy" Chicken Broth (page 19)

18 ounces Basic Ramen Noodles (page 43 or store-bought) or 12 ounces dried ramen noodles

¼ cup butter

¼ cup sliced scallions, green and white parts

1. Fill a medium saucepan with about 4 inches of water and bring to a boil over high heat. Reduce the heat to medium, add the clams, cover, and cook for about 10 minutes, until most of the clam shells have opened (discard any that haven't opened). Use a slotted spoon to remove the clams from the pot. Set aside.

2. Spoon 2 tablespoons of the tare into each of 4 serving bowls.

3. In a large saucepan, heat the "Creamy" Chicken Broth over high heat until it is just about to boil.

4. Cook the noodles according to the recipe (or package instructions) and then drain well.

5. When the noodles are done cooking, immediately ladle the hot soup into the serving bowls over the tare. Add ¼ of the noodles to each bowl. Stir gently and lift with chopsticks to distribute the tare into the broth and to coat the noodles. The noodles should float on top somewhat.

6. Top each bowl with 1 tablespoon of butter, several clams, and 1 tablespoon of the scallions. Serve immediately.

SHIO RAMEN WITH CRISPY FRIED SQUID,
SQUID INK, AND SALMON ROE, PAGE 122

SHIO RAMEN

Shio Ramen with Grilled
Five-Spice Beef Short Ribs,
Corn, and Arugula 120

Shio Ramen with Crispy
Fried Squid, Squid Ink,
and Salmon Roe 122

Shio Ramen with Chashu
Pork Belly, Clams, and
Black Truffle Oil 123

Shiitake Shio Ramen with
Crab, Corn, and Pickled
Daikon Radish 124

Shio Ramen with Ginger
Chicken, Soy Sauce
Eggs, and Yuzu 125

Shiitake Shio Ramen with
Silken Tofu, Mushrooms,
and Crispy Shallots 127

Shio Ramen with Corn,
Roasted Tomatoes,
and Basil 129

Spring Shio Ramen with
Baby Bok Choy, Peas, and
Soft-Boiled Eggs 130

Hakodate Shio Ramen with
Spicy Ground Chicken 131

Shio Ramen with
Grilled Flank Steak
and Chimichurri 132

Shio Ramen with Duck,
Soy Sauce Eggs, and
Bean Sprouts 134

Shio Ramen with Salt
Cod Croquettes and
Soft-Boiled Eggs 135

Shio Ramen with Chicken
Chashu, Cilantro, Lime,
Chiles, and Bean Sprouts 137

Italian Ramen with Chicken,
Soft-Boiled Eggs, Basil,
and Pecorino 138

SHIO RAMEN WITH GRILLED FIVE-SPICE BEEF SHORT RIBS, CORN, AND ARUGULA

NUT-FREE

PREP TIME: 15 minutes, plus overnight to marinate / **COOK TIME:** 2 hours 30 minutes

SERVES 4

When braised for hours, beef short ribs become super tender. Flavored with Chinese five-spice powder, they turn this simple ramen with sweet corn and peppery arugula into a decadent meal.

FOR THE BEEF

1 tablespoon Chinese five-spice powder

1½ teaspoons salt

1 teaspoon sugar

1 teaspoon ground white pepper

2 pounds bone-in beef short ribs

2 tablespoons vegetable oil

1 onion, diced

2 garlic cloves, minced

3 tablespoons mirin

3 tablespoons soy sauce

3 tablespoons rice wine vinegar

2 tablespoons sesame oil

2 teaspoons chili paste

1 tablespoon grated fresh ginger

TO MAKE THE BEEF

1. In a small bowl, combine the five-spice powder, salt, sugar, and white pepper. Rub the mixture all over the ribs. Cover and marinate in the refrigerator overnight.

2. In a Dutch oven, heat the oil over medium-high heat until it shimmers. Working in batches, brown the ribs on all sides, about 10 minutes total. Remove the browned ribs from the pot and add the onion and garlic. Cook, stirring occasionally, until softened, about 5 minutes.

3. Add the mirin and cook, scraping up the browned bits from the pan, for 2 minutes. Return the beef to the pan and add the soy sauce, rice wine vinegar, sesame oil, chili paste, and ginger. Reduce the heat to medium-low, cover the pan, and simmer for about 2 hours, until the meat falls off the bone and is very tender.

FOR THE RAMEN

½ cup Shio Tare (page 33)

8 cups Clear Chicken Broth (page 17)

18 ounces Basic Ramen Noodles (page 43 or store-bought) or 12 ounces dried ramen noodles

1 cup fresh corn kernels (from 2 ears of corn)

2 cups arugula

TO MAKE THE RAMEN

1. Spoon 2 tablespoons of the tare into each of 4 serving bowls.

2. In a large saucepan, heat the Clear Chicken Broth over high heat until it is just about to boil.

3. Cook the noodles according to the recipe (or package instructions) and then drain well.

4. When the noodles are done cooking, immediately ladle the hot soup into the serving bowls over the tare. Add ¼ of the noodles to each bowl. Stir gently and lift with chopsticks to coat the noodles. The noodles should float on top somewhat.

5. Top each bowl with ¼ of the beef, ¼ cup of the corn, and ½ cup of the arugula. Serve immediately.

SHIO RAMEN WITH CRISPY FRIED SQUID, SQUID INK, AND SALMON ROE

DAIRY-FREE, NUT-FREE

PREP TIME: 15 minutes / **COOK TIME:** 15 minutes

SERVES 4

Seafood figures prominently in Japanese cuisine, and this ramen dresses up a simple shio and chicken broth base with Crispy Fried Squid, squid ink, and salmon roe for an aquatic flavor adventure.

½ cup Shio Tare (page 33)

8 cups Clear Chicken Broth (page 17)

2 teaspoons squid ink

18 ounces Basic Ramen Noodles (page 43 or store-bought) or 12 ounces dried ramen noodles

Crispy Fried Squid (page 191)

2 ounces salmon roe

2 cups arugula

1. Spoon 2 tablespoons of the tare into each of 4 serving bowls.

2. In a large saucepan, heat the Clear Chicken Broth over high heat until it is just about to boil. Remove from the heat and immediately stir in the squid ink.

3. Cook the noodles according to the recipe (or package instructions) and then drain well.

4. When the noodles are done cooking, immediately ladle the hot soup into the serving bowls over the tare. Add ¼ of the noodles to each bowl. Stir gently and lift with chopsticks to distribute the tare into the broth and to coat the noodles. The noodles should float on top somewhat.

5. Top each bowl with ¼ of the Crispy Fried Squid, ¼ of the salmon roe, and ½ cup of the arugula. Serve immediately.

Ingredient Tip: *You can buy squid ink from a good grocery store and many specialty food markets. Salmon roe is available frozen from Japanese markets.*

SHIO RAMEN WITH CHASHU PORK BELLY, CLAMS, AND BLACK TRUFFLE OIL

DAIRY-FREE, NUT-FREE

PREP TIME: 15 minutes / **COOK TIME:** 25 minutes

SERVES 4

Delicate littleneck clams and savory Chashu Pork Belly top this "surf and turf" ramen. Earthy black truffle oil is an unconventional addition, but the truffle's umami is a perfect match for the clams and pork.

1 pound live littleneck clams, scrubbed clean

½ cup Shio Tare (page 33)

8 cups Tonkotsu (page 21)

2 tablespoons neutral-flavored vegetable oil

12 slices Chashu Pork Belly (page 49)

18 ounces Basic Ramen Noodles (page 43 or store-bought) or 12 ounces dried ramen noodles

2 teaspoons black truffle oil

1 cup microgreens

1. In a medium saucepan, bring about 4 inches of water to a boil over high heat. Reduce the heat to medium, add the clams, cover, and cook for about 10 minutes, until most of the clam shells have opened (discard any that haven't opened). Use a slotted spoon to remove the clams from the pot. Set aside.

2. Spoon 2 tablespoons of the tare into each of 4 serving bowls.

3. In a large saucepan, heat the Tonkotsu over high heat until it is just about to boil.

4. While the broth is heating, heat the vegetable oil in a skillet and warm the pork slices in it for 1 to 2 minutes on each side.

5. Cook the noodles according to the recipe (or package instructions) and then drain well.

6. When the noodles are done cooking, immediately ladle the hot soup into the serving bowls over the tare. Add ¼ of the noodles to each bowl. Stir gently and lift with chopsticks to distribute the tare into the broth and to coat the noodles. The noodles should float on top somewhat.

7. Top each bowl with several clams, 3 slices of pork, ½ teaspoon of black truffle oil, and ¼ cup of the microgreens. Serve immediately.

Ingredient Tip: *You can find black truffle oil in specialty markets or online. Just be sure the product you're buying contains actual truffles and not synthetic flavorings (called "truffle essence" or "truffle aroma").*

SHIITAKE SHIO RAMEN WITH CRAB, CORN, AND PICKLED DAIKON RADISH

NUT-FREE

PREP TIME: 15 minutes / **COOK TIME:** 20 minutes

SERVES 4

Japanese chefs are focused on using fresh, local ingredients, and I especially love this ramen because it features Dungeness crab, one of my favorite local San Francisco delicacies. You can find Pickled Daikon Radish at Asian markets or, better yet, make it yourself (page 59)!

1 tablespoon butter

4 ounces fresh shiitake mush-rooms, sliced

1 garlic clove, minced

Pinch salt

½ cup Shio Tare (page 33)

8 cups Awase Dashi (page 25)

18 ounces Basic Ramen Noodles (page 43 or store-bought) or 12 ounces dried ramen noodles

1 cup cooked lump Dungeness crab meat

1 cup fresh corn kernels (from 2 ears of corn)

12 slices Pickled Daikon Radish (page 59)

1. In a large skillet, melt the butter over medium-high heat until it bubbles. Add the mushrooms, garlic, and salt and cook, stirring occasionally, until the mushrooms are softened, about 5 minutes.

2. Spoon 2 tablespoons of the tare into each of 4 serving bowls.

3. In a large saucepan, heat the Awase Dashi over high heat until it is just about to boil.

4. Cook the noodles according to the recipe (or package instructions) and then drain well.

5. When the noodles are done cooking, immediately ladle the hot soup into the serving bowls over the tare. Add ¼ of the noodles to each bowl. Stir gently and lift with chopsticks to distribute the tare into the broth and to coat the noodles. The noodles should float on top somewhat.

6. Top each bowl with ¼ cup of the crab meat, ¼ cup of the corn, ¼ of the mushrooms, and 3 slices of the pickled daikon radish. Serve immediately.

SHIO RAMEN WITH GINGER CHICKEN, SOY SAUCE EGGS, AND YUZU

DAIRY-FREE, NUT-FREE

PREP TIME: 15 minutes, plus 30 minutes to marinate / **COOK TIME:** 20 minutes

SERVES 4

Yuzu is a small citrus fruit grown mostly in Japan, Korea, and China. Extremely sour, it's rarely eaten whole, yet its juice and zest add sour notes to cooking, much like lemon. The brightness it adds to this bowl counterbalances the ginger chicken.

FOR THE CHICKEN

1½ tablespoons soy sauce

1½ tablespoons sake

1½ tablespoons honey

1 tablespoon grated fresh ginger

1 pound boneless chicken thighs, cut into bite-size pieces

1 tablespoon neutral-flavored vegetable oil

FOR THE RAMEN

½ cup Shio Tare (page 33)

2 tablespoons yuzu juice

8 cups Clear Chicken Broth (page 17)

18 ounces Basic Ramen Noodles (page 43 or store-bought) or 12 ounces dried ramen noodles

2 Soy Sauce Eggs (page 56), halved lengthwise

¼ cup sliced scallions, green and white parts

TO MAKE THE CHICKEN

1. In a medium mixing bowl, whisk together the soy sauce, sake, honey, and ginger. Add the chicken and toss to coat well. Cover and refrigerate for 30 minutes.

2. In a large skillet, heat the vegetable oil over medium heat until it shimmers. Add the chicken and cook, stirring occasionally, until the chicken is browned on all sides, 5 to 7 minutes.

3. Add the marinade to the pan and cook, stirring, to coat the chicken. Let simmer for 1 to 2 minutes, until the sauce thickens a bit.

TO MAKE THE RAMEN

1. Spoon 2 tablespoons of the tare into each of 4 serving bowls. Add 1½ teaspoons of yuzu juice to each bowl.

2. In a large saucepan, heat the Clear Chicken Broth over high heat until it is just about to boil.

3. Cook the noodles according to the recipe (or package instructions) and then drain well.

4. When the noodles are done cooking, immediately ladle the hot soup into the serving bowls over the tare and yuzu juice. Add ¼ of the noodles to each bowl. Stir gently and lift with chopsticks to distribute the tare into the broth and to coat the noodles. The noodles should float on top somewhat.

Continued

5. Top each bowl with ¼ of the chicken, half of 1 egg, and 1 table-spoon of the scallions. Serve immediately.

~~~~~~~~~~~~~~~~~~~~~~~~~~~~~~~~

Ingredient Tip: *Fresh, whole yuzu is nearly impossible to find in the United States, but you can buy bottled juice in Asian markets. For this recipe, be sure to buy pure, unsweetened yuzu juice (which may also be sold as citron juice in some markets).*

~~~~~~~~~~~~~~~~~~~~~~~~~~~~~~~~

SHIITAKE SHIO RAMEN WITH SILKEN TOFU, MUSHROOMS, AND CRISPY SHALLOTS

DAIRY-FREE, NUT-FREE, VEGAN

PREP TIME: 15 minutes / **COOK TIME:** 20 minutes

SERVES 4

This vegan ramen starts with an umami-rich Shiitake Dashi. Sautéed shiitakes, silken tofu, and crispy shallots provide lots of flavor and texture. This quick "fry" method is pure perfection, saving both time and mess.

3 tablespoons neutral-flavored vegetable oil, divided

4 ounces fresh shiitake mushrooms, sliced

1 garlic clove, minced

Pinch salt

1 medium shallot, thinly sliced

½ cup Shio Tare (page 33)

8 cups Shiitake Dashi (page 26)

18 ounces Basic Ramen Noodles (page 43 or store-bought) or 12 ounces dried ramen noodles

6 ounces silken tofu, diced

1. In a large skillet, heat 1 tablespoon of vegetable oil over medium-high heat until it shimmers. Add the mushrooms, garlic, and salt and cook, stirring occasionally, until the mushrooms are softened, about 5 minutes.

2. In a small bowl, toss the shallot with the remaining 2 tablespoons of vegetable oil. Spread the shallot slices out into a single layer on a microwave-safe plate. Microwave in 30-second intervals, until the shallots turn golden brown, about 2 minutes total. Stop cooking when they are mostly brown, but not too dark. Keep in mind that they will continue to cook after being removed from the microwave because the oil will be very hot.

3. Spoon 2 tablespoons of the tare into each of 4 serving bowls.

4. In a large saucepan, heat the Shiitake Dashi over high heat until it is just about to boil.

5. Cook the noodles according to the recipe (or package instructions) and then drain well.

6. When the noodles are done cooking, immediately ladle the hot soup into the serving bowls over the tare. Add ¼ of the noodles to each bowl. Stir gently and lift with chopsticks to distribute the tare into the broth and to coat the noodles. The noodles should float on top somewhat.

Continued

7. Top each bowl with ¼ of the tofu, ¼ of the mushrooms, and ¼ of the shallots. Serve immediately.

Repurposing Tip: *Make a big batch of the fried shallots, then use them to add crunch to salads, soups, or stir-fries, or to top steamed rice.*

SHIO RAMEN WITH CORN, ROASTED TOMATOES, AND BASIL

DAIRY-FREE, NUT-FREE

PREP TIME: 15 minutes / **COOK TIME:** 15 minutes

SERVES 4

Topping ramen with roasted tomatoes is an idea borrowed from the only American-born ramen master, Ivan Orkin. The non-native ingredient is unexpected, but adds luscious texture. Pairing tomatoes with fresh corn and basil makes this a bright summer-in-a-bowl ramen.

½ cup Shio Tare (page 33)

4 teaspoons Scallion Oil (page 40)

8 cups Awase Dashi (page 25)

18 ounces Basic Ramen Noodles (page 43 or store-bought) or 12 ounces dried ramen noodles

Roasted Tomatoes (page 61)

1 cup fresh corn kernels (from 2 ears of corn)

¼ cup julienned fresh basil

1. Spoon 2 tablespoons of the tare into each of 4 serving bowls. Add 1 teaspoon of Scallion Oil to each.

2. In a large saucepan, heat the Awase Dashi over high heat until it is just about to boil.

3. Cook the noodles according to the recipe (or package instructions) and then drain well.

4. When the noodles are done cooking, immediately ladle the hot soup into the serving bowls over the tare and oil. Add ¼ of the noodles to each bowl. Stir gently and lift with chopsticks to distribute the tare into the broth and to coat the noodles. The noodles should float on top somewhat.

5. Top each bowl with 2 or 3 tomato halves, ¼ cup of the corn, and 1 tablespoon of basil. Serve immediately.

SPRING SHIO RAMEN WITH BABY BOK CHOY, PEAS, AND SOFT-BOILED EGGS

DAIRY-FREE, NUT-FREE, VEGETARIAN

PREP TIME: 15 minutes / **COOK TIME:** 20 minutes

SERVES 4

This simple ramen showcases some of the best springtime produce. With a base of earthy Shiitake Dashi and a pile of wholesome veggies, it's delicious and beautiful with an array of green from the peas, shoots, bok choy, and scallions.

1 tablespoon sesame oil

2 garlic cloves, minced

2 teaspoons grated fresh ginger

4 scallions, sliced, green and white parts separated

⅓ pound baby bok choy

12 ounces shelled English peas

½ cup Shio Tare (page 33)

4 teaspoons Scallion Oil (page 40)

8 cups Shiitake Dashi (page 26)

18 ounces Basic Ramen Noodles (page 43 or store-bought) or 12 ounces dried ramen noodles

2 Soft-Boiled Eggs (page 55), halved lengthwise

2 ounces pea shoots

1. In a large skillet, heat the sesame oil over medium heat until it shimmers. Add the garlic, ginger, and scallion whites. Cook, stirring frequently, until fragrant, about 1 minute. Add the baby bok choy and peas and cook, stirring occasionally, for about 2 minutes more, until wilted. Remove from the heat.

2. Spoon 2 tablespoons of the tare into each of 4 serving bowls. Add 1 teaspoon of Scallion Oil to each bowl.

3. In a large saucepan, heat the Shiitake Dashi over high heat until it is just about to boil.

4. Cook the noodles according to the recipe (or package instructions) and then drain well.

5. When the noodles are done cooking, immediately ladle the hot soup into the serving bowls over the tare and oil. Add ¼ of the noodles to each bowl. Stir gently and lift with chopsticks to distribute the tare into the broth and to coat the noodles. The noodles should float on top somewhat.

6. Top each bowl with half of 1 Soft-Boiled Egg, ¼ of the bok choy and peas mixture, ¼ of the scallion greens, and ¼ of the pea shoots. Serve immediately.

Substitution Tip: *To make this vegan, omit the Soft-Boiled Eggs. For added protein, add diced silken tofu, if you like.*

HAKODATE SHIO RAMEN WITH SPICY GROUND CHICKEN

DAIRY-FREE, NUT-FREE

PREP TIME: 15 minutes / **COOK TIME:** 20 minutes

SERVES 4

In Hakodate, ramen is seasoned with Shio Tare and usually includes kombu in the broth. This version uses a combination of Clear Chicken Broth and Awase Dashi. The ground chicken topping is quick to make and adds savory heft.

1 pound ground chicken

½ teaspoon salt

1 garlic clove, minced

1 teaspoon soy sauce

1 tablespoon Chili Oil (page 39)

½ cup Shio Tare (page 33)

6 cups Clear Chicken Broth (page 17)

2 cups Awase Dashi (page 25)

18 ounces Basic Ramen Noodles (page 43 or store-bought) or 12 ounces dried ramen noodles

¼ cup sliced scallions, green and white parts

1. Heat a large skillet over medium-high heat. Add the chicken and salt and cook, stirring occasionally and breaking up with a spatula, until the meat is browned, about 5 minutes.

2. Add the garlic and cook, stirring, for 1 minute more. Stir in the soy sauce and remove from the heat. Stir in the Chili Oil.

3. Spoon 2 tablespoons of the tare into each of 4 serving bowls.

4. In a large saucepan, combine the Clear Chicken Broth and Awase Dashi and heat over high heat until it is just about to boil.

5. Cook the noodles according to the recipe (or package instructions) and then drain well.

6. When the noodles are done cooking, immediately ladle the hot soup into the serving bowls over the tare. Add ¼ of the noodles to each bowl. Stir gently and lift with chopsticks to distribute the tare into the broth and to coat the noodles. The noodles should float on top somewhat.

7. Top each bowl with ¼ of the chicken mixture and 1 tablespoon of the scallions and serve immediately.

Substitution Tip: *Make this vegan by substituting crumbled firm tofu for the chicken and omitting the Clear Chicken Broth (use 8 cups of the Shiitake Dashi (page 26)).*

SHIO RAMEN WITH GRILLED FLANK STEAK AND CHIMICHURRI

DAIRY-FREE, NUT-FREE

PREP TIME: 15 minutes / **COOK TIME:** 45 minutes

SERVES 4

Ramen is endlessly flexible and adaptable to different cooking styles and ingredients. Chimichurri is an Argentinean oil-based sauce of chopped fresh herbs and garlic, and matches perfectly with grilled meat (its usual foil in Argentina!). Here, the flank steak's smokiness marries with Shio Tare, Clear Chicken Broth, and chewy, slurpable noodles for a wonderfully balanced bowl.

FOR THE CHIMICHURRI

¼ cup extra-virgin olive oil

1 tablespoon red wine vinegar

¼ cup finely chopped flat-leaf parsley

2 garlic cloves, minced

1 small, hot red chile (any type), seeded and finely chopped

½ teaspoon kosher salt

¼ teaspoon freshly ground black pepper

FOR THE STEAK

1 pound flank steak

Kosher salt

Freshly ground black pepper

FOR THE RAMEN

½ cup Shio Tare (page 33)

8 cups Clear Chicken Broth (page 17)

18 ounces Basic Ramen Noodles (page 43 or store-bought) or 12 ounces dried ramen noodles

TO MAKE THE CHIMICHURRI

In a small bowl, stir together the olive oil, red wine vinegar, parsley, garlic, chile, salt, and pepper. Set aside.

TO MAKE THE STEAK

1. Heat a grill or grill pan to medium-high heat.

2. Season the steak generously with salt and pepper. Grill to desired doneness, about 5 minutes per side for medium-rare. Remove the steak from the heat and let rest for 10 minutes before slicing across the grain into ¼-inch-thick slices.

TO MAKE THE RAMEN

1. Spoon 2 tablespoons of the tare into each of 4 serving bowls.

2. In a large saucepan, heat the Clear Chicken Broth over high heat until it is just about to boil.

3. Cook the noodles according to the recipe (or package instructions) and then drain well.

4. When the noodles are done cooking, immediately ladle the hot soup into the serving bowls over the tare. Add ¼ of the noodles to each bowl. Stir gently and lift with chopsticks to distribute the tare into the broth and to coat the noodles. The noodles should float on top somewhat.

5. Top each bowl with several slices of steak and a generous dollop of the chimichurri. Serve immediately.

Substitution Tip: *Chimichurri can be made with a variety of herbs. Feel free to use cilantro, basil, oregano, or shiso.*

SHIO RAMEN WITH DUCK, SOY SAUCE EGGS, AND BEAN SPROUTS

DAIRY-FREE, NUT-FREE

PREP TIME: 15 minutes / **COOK TIME:** 45 minutes

SERVES 4

Duck is a fun change from the usual chicken. Meatier than white-meat chicken, the duck breast gets a crispy skin here, making it a decadent topping for this otherwise simple ramen.

2 duck breasts, scored through the skin several times

Kosher salt

Freshly ground black pepper

½ cup Shio Tare (page 33)

8 cups Clear Chicken Broth (page 17)

18 ounces Basic Ramen Noodles (page 43 or store-bought) or 12 ounces dried ramen noodles

¼ cup sliced scallions, green and white parts

1 cup bean sprouts

2 Soy Sauce Eggs (page 56), halved lengthwise

1. Season the duck generously with salt and pepper.

2. Heat a large skillet over medium heat. Add the duck breasts, skin-side down and cook for 20 to 25 minutes, until the skin is crispy and well-browned and the fat has rendered completely. Turn the breasts over and cook for about 5 minutes on the second side. Remove the duck from the pan (reserve the rendered fat) and let rest for 10 minutes before slicing into ¼-inch-thick slices.

3. Spoon 2 tablespoons of the tare into each of 4 serving bowls.

4. In a large saucepan, heat the Clear Chicken Broth over high heat until it is just about to boil.

5. Cook the noodles according to the recipe (or package instructions) and then drain well.

6. When the noodles are done cooking, immediately ladle the hot soup into the serving bowls over the tare. Add ¼ of the noodles to each bowl. Stir gently and lift with chopsticks to distribute the tare into the broth and to coat the noodles. The noodles should float on top somewhat.

7. Top each bowl with several slices of duck, 1 tablespoon of the scallions, ¼ cup of the bean sprouts, and half of 1 egg. Add 1 teaspoon of the rendered duck fat to each bowl, if desired. Serve immediately.

Substitution Tip: *If you happen to have duck broth in your freezer, go ahead and use it instead of the Clear Chicken Broth.*

SHIO RAMEN WITH SALT COD CROQUETTES AND SOFT-BOILED EGGS

DAIRY-FREE, NUT-FREE

PREP TIME: 15 minutes, plus 24 hours to soak and 30 minutes to chill / **COOK TIME:** 45 minutes

SERVES 4

Brazil has the largest expat Japanese population in the world, and everywhere ramen travels, it gets a local twist. Salt cod is a staple in Brazilian cuisine, and you'll see cod croquettes being sold out of street stalls and as a bar snack. They're a great topper for ramen—São Paulo style!

FOR THE CROQUETTES

¾ pound salt cod

2 tablespoons extra-virgin olive oil

½ onion, finely diced

1 pound potatoes, boiled and mashed

1 large egg

1 tablespoon fresh cilantro

Pinch kosher salt

Neutral-flavored vegetable oil, for frying

FOR THE RAMEN

½ cup Shio Tare (page 33)

8 cups Clear Chicken Broth (page 17)

18 ounces Basic Ramen Noodles (page 43 or store-bought) or 12 ounces dried ramen noodles

2 Soft-Boiled Eggs (page 55), halved lengthwise

¼ cup sliced scallions, green and white parts

TO MAKE THE CROQUETTES

1. Rinse the cod and then soak it in cold water for 24 hours, changing the water 2 or 3 times.

2. Drain the cod and place it in a medium saucepan. Cover with cold water. Bring the water to a simmer over medium-high heat, then reduce the heat to low and simmer for 15 minutes.

3. Drain the fish and then set aside to cool. When cool enough to handle, discard the skin and any bones you can find in the flesh while breaking the fish apart with your fingers.

4. In a small skillet, heat the olive oil over medium-high heat. Add the onion and cook, stirring, until softened, about 5 minutes.

5. In a medium mixing bowl, stir together the cod, onion, potatoes, egg, cilantro, and salt.

6. Form the mixture into 8 oblong balls using your hands. Place the balls on a plate in a single layer and refrigerate for 20 to 30 minutes to help them set.

7. Fill a deep, heavy pot with about 3 inches of vegetable oil and heat it over high heat until it shimmers. Cook the croquettes a few at a time, turning once, until they are deep golden brown all over, about 2 to 3 minutes. Transfer the cooked croquettes to a paper towel–lined plate to drain.

Continued

TO MAKE THE RAMEN

1. Spoon 2 tablespoons of the tare into each of 4 serving bowls.

2. In a large saucepan, heat the Clear Chicken Broth over high heat until it is just about to boil.

3. Cook the noodles according to the recipe (or package instructions) and then drain well.

4. When the noodles are done cooking, immediately ladle the hot soup into the serving bowls over the tare. Add ¼ of the noodles to each bowl. Stir gently and lift with chopsticks to distribute the tare into the broth and to coat the noodles. The noodles should float on top somewhat.

5. Top each bowl with 2 croquettes, half of 1 Soft-Boiled Egg, and 1 tablespoon of the scallions. Serve immediately.

Prep-Ahead Tip: *Although somewhat laborious to make, croquettes freeze well. Make a batch in advance and when you're ready to serve them, you can fry them straight from the freezer.*

SHIO RAMEN WITH CHICKEN CHASHU, CILANTRO, LIME, CHILES, AND BEAN SPROUTS

DAIRY-FREE, NUT-FREE

PREP TIME: 15 minutes / **COOK TIME:** 15 minutes

SERVES 4

This recipe demonstrates the adaptability of ramen. Chile, lime, and cilantro aren't ingredients you often find in Japanese cuisine, but put them on a bowl of "Creamy" Chicken Broth, seasoned with Shio Tare and topped with slices of Chicken Chashu, and they seem right at home.

½ cup Shio Tare (page 33)

8 cups "Creamy" Chicken Broth (page 19)

2 tablespoons neutral-flavored vegetable oil

12 slices Chicken Chashu (page 53)

18 ounces Basic Ramen Noodles (page 43 or store-bought) or 12 ounces dried ramen noodles

¼ cup chopped fresh cilantro

1 jalapeño pepper, cut into thin rounds

1 cup bean sprouts

1 lime, quartered

1. Spoon 2 tablespoons of the tare into each of 4 serving bowls.

2. In a large saucepan, heat the "Creamy" Chicken Broth over high heat until you see bubbles around the edges and it is just about to boil.

3. While the broth is heating, heat the vegetable oil in a skillet and warm the chicken slices in it for 1 to 2 minutes on each side.

4. Cook the noodles according to the recipe (or package instructions) and then drain well.

5. When the noodles are finished cooking, immediately ladle the hot broth into the serving bowls over the tare. Add ¼ of the noodles to each bowl. Stir gently and lift with chopsticks to distribute the tare into the broth and to coat the noodles. The noodles should float on top somewhat.

6. Top each bowl with 3 slices of chicken, 1 tablespoon of the cilantro, ¼ of the jalapeño rounds, and ¼ cup of the bean sprouts. Set a lime wedge on the side of each bowl for diners to squeeze into their soup as they choose. Serve immediately.

ITALIAN RAMEN WITH CHICKEN, SOFT-BOILED EGGS, BASIL, AND PECORINO

NUT-FREE

PREP TIME: 15 minutes / **COOK TIME:** 15 minutes

SERVES 4

This Italian version proves, once again, that ramen makes itself quite comfortable wherever it goes. The basil's freshness and the pecorino cheese's pungency scream Italy, but they also blend seamlessly with the deep umami of the "Creamy" Chicken Broth and Shio Tare.

½ cup Shio Tare (page 33)

8 cups "Creamy" Chicken Broth (page 19)

18 ounces Basic Ramen Noodles (page 43 or store-bought) or 12 ounces dried ramen noodles

1 pound shredded cooked chicken

2 Soft-Boiled Eggs (page 55), halved lengthwise

¼ cup julienned fresh basil

½ cup shaved pecorino cheese

1. Spoon 2 tablespoons of the tare into each of 4 serving bowls.

2. In a large saucepan, heat the "Creamy" Chicken Broth over high heat until you see bubbles around the edges and it is just about to boil.

3. Cook the noodles according to the recipe (or package instructions) and then drain well.

4. When the noodles are finished cooking, immediately ladle the hot broth into the serving bowls over the tare. Add ¼ of the noodles to each bowl. Stir gently and lift with chopsticks to distribute the tare into the broth and to coat the noodles. The noodles should float on top somewhat.

5. Top each bowl with ¼ of the chicken, half of 1 Soft-Boiled Egg, 1 tablespoon of the basil, and 2 tablespoons of the pecorino cheese. Serve immediately.

Ingredient Tip: *Use leftover roast chicken or pick up a rotisserie chicken at your supermarket.*

SOY SAUCE EGGS, PAGE 56

MISO RAMEN

Miso Pumpkin Ramen
with Pan-Fried Tofu
and Bok Choy 142

Miso Ramen with Crispy
Pork Katsu and Black
Garlic Oil 144

Creamy Miso Chicken Ramen
with Chashu Pork Belly and
Maitake Mushrooms 145

Miso Ramen with Ginger Pork
and Roasted Vegetables 146

Spicy Miso Ramen with
Chicken Karaage and
Swiss Chard 148

Miso Ramen with Spicy
Garlic Paste, Chicken,
and Cilantro 149

Miso-Ginger Ramen
with Spinach and
Seared Salmon 150

Creamy Miso Ramen with
Broiled Cod, Scallions, and
Kikurage Mushrooms 151

Spicy Miso Ramen with
Brussels Sprouts, Shiitake
Mushrooms, and Bacon 153

Miso Ramen with Roasted
Tomato, Bacon, and Egg 154

Miso Ramen with Shaved
Asparagus, Scallions,
and Lemon Zest 155

Miso Ramen with Kimchi,
Shiitake Mushrooms, and
Soy Sauce Eggs 156

Spicy Miso Ramen with
Corn, Butter, Spinach, and
Soy Sauce Eggs 157

Miso Ramen with Smoky
Eggplant, Ginger,
and Spinach 158

Soy Milk Miso Ramen with
Yuba, Shiitake Mushrooms,
and Pickled Ginger 159

Miso Ramen with Pan-Fried
Tofu, Kabocha Squash,
and Baby Bok Choy 160

MISO PUMPKIN RAMEN WITH PAN-FRIED TOFU AND BOK CHOY

DAIRY-FREE, NUT-FREE, VEGAN

PREP TIME: 15 minutes / **COOK TIME:** 1 hour

SERVES 4

Kabocha squash is a Japanese pumpkin with a velvety texture and sweet flavor, especially when roasted. Tossing it with an umami-loaded mixture of miso and shoyu intensifies the flavors, making it an ideal topping for a vegan ramen. Pan-fried tofu, fresh corn, and baby bok choy complement the squash, certifying this soup as a deeply satisfying meal.

FOR THE BROTH

4 cups Shiitake Dashi
  (page 26)
1 tablespoon minced
  fresh ginger
2 garlic cloves, crushed

TO MAKE THE BROTH

In a stockpot, combine the Shiitake Dashi, ginger, and garlic and bring to a boil over high heat. Immediately lower the heat to medium-low and simmer for 30 minutes.

FOR THE RAMEN AND TOPPINGS

2 tablespoons neutral-flavored vegetable oil

¾ cup firm tofu, cut into small rectangles

Kosher salt

12 ounces Basic Ramen Noodles (page 43 or store-bought) or 5 ounces dried ramen noodles

⅓ pound baby bok choy

½ cup white miso

2 tablespoons shoyu

1 scallion, chopped, green and white parts

½ cup fresh corn kernels, cut from an ear of corn

Roasted Kabocha Squash (page 60)

1 tablespoon toasted sesame seeds

TO MAKE THE RAMEN AND TOPPINGS

1. In a medium nonstick skillet, heat the vegetable oil over medium-high heat until it shimmers. Add the tofu, seasoning liberally with salt, and cook, stirring frequently, until browned, about 5 minutes.

2. Cook the noodles according to the package or recipe directions and then drain.

3. Remove the broth mixture from the heat and stir in the bok choy, miso, shoyu, and scallions.

4. Ladle the broth into serving bowls. Add ¼ of the noodles to each bowl. Stir gently and lift with chopsticks to coat the noodles. The noodles should float on top somewhat.

5. Top with equal portions of tofu, bok choy, corn, kabocha squash, and sesame seeds.

Ingredient Tip: *You can find kabocha squash in Asian markets and some supermarkets or farmers' markets. If you can't find it, you can substitute sugar pumpkin or butternut squash.*

MISO RAMEN WITH CRISPY PORK KATSU AND BLACK GARLIC OIL

DAIRY-FREE, NUT-FREE

PREP TIME: 15 minutes / **COOK TIME:** 15 minutes

SERVES 4

Although this is a very simple ramen, it is anything but dull. The pork's crispy crunch gives textural balance to the tender noodles, and the smoky bitterness of the Black Garlic Oil ties it all together.

½ cup Miso Tare (page 30)

4 teaspoons Black Garlic Oil (page 38)

8 cups Clear Chicken Broth (page 17)

18 ounces Basic Ramen Noodles (page 43 or store-bought) or 12 ounces dried ramen noodles

Pork Katsu (page 52)

2 Soft-Boiled Eggs (page 55), halved lengthwise

1. Spoon 2 tablespoons of the tare into each of 4 serving bowls. Add 1 teaspoon of Black Garlic Oil to each bowl.

2. In a large saucepan, heat the Clear Chicken Broth over high heat until you see bubbles around the edges and it is just about to boil.

3. Cook the noodles according to the recipe (or package instructions) and then drain well.

4. When the noodles are finished cooking, immediately ladle the hot broth into the serving bowls over the tare and oil. Add ¼ of the noodles to each bowl. Stir gently and lift with chopsticks to distribute the tare and oil into the broth and to coat the noodles. The noodles should float on top somewhat.

5. Top each bowl with ¼ of the pork and half of 1 Soft-Boiled Egg. Serve immediately.

CREAMY MISO CHICKEN RAMEN WITH CHASHU PORK BELLY AND MAITAKE MUSHROOMS

DAIRY-FREE, NUT-FREE

PREP TIME: 15 minutes / **COOK TIME:** 30 minutes

SERVES 4

Maitake mushrooms (also known as hen of the woods) have leaf-like, delicate caps and are succulent when cooked, with a spicy, earthy flavor. Roasting gives them an especially appealing texture: meaty, chewy, and crisp around the edges.

8 ounces maitake mushrooms, split into small clumps

2 tablespoons extra-virgin olive oil

Kosher salt

Freshly ground black pepper

½ cup Miso Tare (page 30)

8 cups "Creamy" Chicken Broth (page 19)

1 tablespoon neutral-flavored vegetable oil

12 slices Chashu Pork Belly (page 49)

18 ounces Basic Ramen Noodles (page 43 or store-bought) or 12 ounces dried ramen noodles

2 Soft-Boiled Eggs (page 55), halved lengthwise

1. Preheat the oven to 400°F.

2. Toss the mushrooms with the olive oil, salt, and pepper. Spread them out onto a foil-lined baking sheet. Roast until the edges are browned and crisp, about 15 minutes.

3. Spoon 2 tablespoons of the tare into each of 4 serving bowls.

4. In a large saucepan, heat the "Creamy" Chicken Broth over high heat until you see bubbles around the edges and it is just about to boil.

5. While the broth is heating, heat the vegetable oil in a skillet and warm the pork slices in it for 1 to 2 minutes on each side.

6. Cook the noodles according to the recipe (or package instructions) and then drain well.

7. When the noodles are finished cooking, immediately ladle the hot broth into the serving bowls over the tare. Add ¼ of the noodles to each bowl. Stir gently and lift with chopsticks to distribute the tare into the broth and to coat the noodles. The noodles should float on top somewhat.

8. Top each bowl with 3 slices of the pork, half of 1 Soft-Boiled Egg, and ¼ of the mushrooms. Serve immediately.

Substitution Tip: *If you don't have maitake mushrooms, substitute sliced shiitakes cooked the same way.*

MISO RAMEN WITH GINGER PORK AND ROASTED VEGETABLES

DAIRY-FREE, NUT-FREE

PREP TIME: 15 minutes / **COOK TIME:** 45 minutes

SERVES 4

This veggie-packed ramen bowl has a lot going on, but comes together with surprising ease if you make the components ahead of time. Put it all together for a very satisfying meal.

FOR THE ROASTED VEGETABLES

3 tablespoons white miso

2 tablespoons soy sauce

3 tablespoons neutral-flavored vegetable oil

2 tablespoons brown sugar

¼ kabocha squash, peeled, seeded, and cut into cubes

⅓ pound broccoli rabe

1 Japanese eggplant, cut into 3-inch-long strips

FOR THE RAMEN

½ cup Miso Tare (page 30)

8 cups Clear Chicken Broth (page 17)

18 ounces Basic Ramen Noodles (page 43 or store-bought) or 12 ounces dried ramen noodles

Ginger Pork (page 50)

TO MAKE THE ROASTED VEGETABLES

1. Preheat the oven to 400°F.

2. In a medium bowl, stir together the white miso, soy sauce, vegetable oil, and brown sugar. Add the squash, broccoli rabe, and eggplant and toss to coat. Spread the vegetables out in a single layer on a baking sheet and roast in the oven for 25 to 30 minutes, until tender and beginning to brown.

TO MAKE THE RAMEN

1. Spoon 2 tablespoons of the tare into each of 4 serving bowls.

2. In a large saucepan, heat the Clear Chicken Broth over high heat until you see bubbles around the edges and it is just about to boil.

3. Cook the noodles according to the recipe (or package instructions) and then drain well.

4. When the noodles are finished cooking, immediately ladle the hot broth into the serving bowls over the tare. Add ¼ of the noodles to each bowl. Stir gently and lift with chopsticks to distribute the tare into the broth and to coat the noodles. The noodles should float on top somewhat.

5. Top each bowl with ¼ of the Ginger Pork and ¼ of the roasted vegetable mixture. Serve immediately.

Prep-Ahead Tip: *The vegetables can be roasted up to 3 days ahead of time. To serve, warm them in a hot oven or in the microwave.*

SPICY MISO RAMEN WITH CHICKEN KARAAGE AND SWISS CHARD

DAIRY-FREE, NUT-FREE

PREP TIME: 15 minutes / **COOK TIME:** 15 minutes

SERVES 4

Chicken Karaage—crispy deep-fried morsels—offers a welcome textural contrast to the tender noodles and rich, miso-tinged broth in this ramen bowl. This is a complex flavor bomb in every possible way and one of my favorite ramens.

2 teaspoons sesame oil

8 ounces Swiss chard, sliced into ribbons

½ cup Spicy Miso Tare (page 31)

¼ cup Rendered Chicken Fat (page 36)

8 cups Clear Chicken Broth (page 17)

18 ounces Basic Ramen Noodles (page 43 or store-bought) or 12 ounces dried ramen noodles

Chicken Karaage (page 54)

2 Soft-Boiled Eggs (page 55), halved lengthwise

2 bunches enoki mushrooms

1. In a large skillet, heat the sesame oil over medium-high heat until it shimmers. Add the Swiss chard and cook, stirring frequently, until wilted, about 3 minutes. Remove the pan from the heat; set aside.

2. Spoon 2 tablespoons of the tare and 1 tablespoon of the fat into each of 4 serving bowls.

3. In a large saucepan, heat the Clear Chicken Broth over high heat until small bubbles form around the edge and it is just about to boil.

4. Cook the noodles according to the recipe (or package instructions) and then drain well.

5. When the noodles are done cooking, immediately ladle the hot soup into the serving bowls over the tare and fat. Add ¼ of the noodles to each bowl. Stir gently and lift with chopsticks to distribute the tare into the broth and to coat the noodles. The noodles should float on top somewhat.

6. Top each bowl with 3 or 4 pieces of the chicken, half of 1 Soft-Boiled Egg, ¼ of the sautéed Swiss chard, and ¼ of the enoki mushrooms. Serve immediately.

Substitution Tip: *If you have Pork Katsu (page 52), feel free to substitute it for the Chicken Karaage here.*

MISO RAMEN WITH SPICY GARLIC PASTE, CHICKEN, AND CILANTRO

DAIRY-FREE

PREP TIME: 15 minutes / **COOK TIME:** 15 minutes

SERVES 4

This bowl is on the lighter side, featuring shredded cooked chicken and fresh cilantro. Spicy garlic paste adds a splash of color and gives it a kick. The Soft-Boiled Eggs supply a much-appreciated richness.

½ cup Miso Tare (page 30)

8 cups Clear Chicken Broth (page 17)

18 ounces Basic Ramen Noodles (page 43 or store-bought) or 12 ounces dried ramen noodles

1 pound shredded cooked chicken

2 Soft-Boiled Eggs (page 55), halved lengthwise

¼ cup chopped fresh cilantro

4 to 8 teaspoons spicy garlic paste

1. Spoon 2 tablespoons of the tare into each of 4 serving bowls.

2. In a large saucepan, heat the Clear Chicken Broth over high heat until small bubbles form around the edge and it is just about to boil.

3. Cook the noodles according to the recipe (or package instructions) and then drain well.

4. When the noodles are done cooking, immediately ladle the hot soup into the serving bowls over the tare. Add ¼ of the noodles to each bowl. Stir gently and lift with chopsticks to distribute the tare into the broth and to coat the noodles. The noodles should float on top somewhat.

5. Top each bowl with ¼ of the chicken, half of 1 Soft-Boiled Egg, 1 tablespoon of the cilantro, and 1 to 2 teaspoons of spicy garlic paste. Serve immediately.

Ingredient Tip: *Spicy garlic paste is a mixture of chiles and garlic that can be found in Asian markets or the Asian foods aisle of most supermarkets.*

MISO-GINGER RAMEN WITH SPINACH AND SEARED SALMON

DAIRY-FREE, NUT-FREE

PREP TIME: 15 minutes / **COOK TIME:** 20 minutes

SERVES 4

One of the things I love about Japanese cuisine is that most of it is super nutritious and this ramen bowl exemplifies that. Salmon and spinach are both packed with nutrients, and play perfectly with a gingery, miso-flavored broth.

1 tablespoon sesame oil

1 pound salmon fillet (see Ingredient Tip)

Kosher salt

Freshly ground black pepper

½ cup Miso Tare (page 30)

2 tablespoons grated fresh ginger

8 cups Clear Chicken Broth (page 17)

2 cups fresh spinach

18 ounces Basic Ramen Noodles (page 43 or store-bought) or 12 ounces dried ramen noodles

¼ cup sliced scallions, green and white parts

1. In a large skillet, heat the sesame oil over medium-high heat. Season the salmon fillet on both sides with salt and pepper and cook for 4 to 6 minutes per side, until the fish is cooked through and browned on the outside.

2. Spoon 2 tablespoons of the tare and 1½ teaspoons of the ginger into each of 4 serving bowls.

3. In a large saucepan, heat the Clear Chicken Broth over high heat until small bubbles form around the edge and it is just about to boil. Add the spinach to the broth and cook until just wilted, about 1 minute. Use a slotted spoon to remove the spinach from the broth. Set aside.

4. Cook the noodles according to the recipe (or package instructions) and then drain well.

5. When the noodles are done cooking, immediately ladle the hot soup into the serving bowls over the tare and ginger. Add ¼ of the noodles to each bowl. Stir gently and lift with chopsticks to distribute the tare into the broth and to coat the noodles. The noodles should float on top somewhat.

6. Top each bowl with ¼ of the salmon, ¼ of the spinach, and 1 tablespoon of the scallions. Serve immediately.

Ingredient Tip: *Choose wild-caught salmon whenever possible, but be careful not to overcook it. Leaner than farmed salmon, it can dry out quickly.*

CREAMY MISO RAMEN WITH BROILED COD, SCALLIONS, AND KIKURAGE MUSHROOMS

DAIRY-FREE, NUT-FREE

PREP TIME: 15 minutes, plus 2 hours to marinate / **COOK TIME:** 20 minutes

SERVES 4

When you broil cod with a miso glaze, it becomes flaky, and the glaze blackens as the sugars caramelize, giving it a concentrated sweet-savory flavor. Kikurage mushrooms, also called wood ear mushrooms, add a pleasing crunch.

FOR THE COD

2 tablespoons sake

2 tablespoons mirin

2 tablespoons white miso paste

1½ tablespoons sugar

1 pound cod fillet

FOR THE RAMEN

½ cup Miso Tare (page 30)

8 cups "Creamy" Chicken Broth (page 19)

18 ounces Basic Ramen Noodles (page 43 or store-bought) or 12 ounces dried ramen noodles

4 ounces dried kikurage mushrooms, rehydrated in warm water, drained, and julienned

¼ cup sliced scallions, green and white parts

TO MAKE THE COD

1. In a small saucepan, combine the sake and mirin and bring to a boil over high heat. Let the mixture boil for about 30 seconds. Reduce the heat to low and whisk in the white miso paste. Once the miso has completely dissolved, raise the heat to high and whisk in the sugar. Cook, whisking constantly, until the sugar is dissolved. Remove from the heat and let cool to room temperature.

2. Spread the miso mixture over the fish, wrap in plastic wrap, and marinate in the refrigerator for at least 2 hours and up to 2 days.

3. When ready to cook the fish, heat the broiler to high. Place the fish on a baking sheet and cook under the broiler until the fish is opaque and flakes easily with a fork and the top is dark brown, and even blackened in some spots, 8 to 10 minutes.

TO MAKE THE RAMEN

1. Spoon 2 tablespoons of the tare into each of 4 serving bowls.

2. In a large saucepan, heat the "Creamy" Chicken Broth over high heat until you see bubbles around the edges and it is just about to boil.

3. Cook the noodles according to the recipe (or package instructions) and then drain well.

Continued

4. When the noodles are finished cooking, immediately ladle the hot broth into the serving bowls over the tare. Add ¼ of the noodles to each bowl. Stir gently and lift with chopsticks to distribute the tare into the broth and to coat the noodles. The noodles should float on top somewhat.

5. Top each bowl with ¼ of the cod, ¼ of the mushrooms, and 1 tablespoon of the scallions. Serve immediately.

Substitution Tip: *This marinade and cooking method work just as well with 1-inch-thick salmon fillets.*

SPICY MISO RAMEN WITH BRUSSELS SPROUTS, SHIITAKE MUSHROOMS, AND BACON

DAIRY-FREE, NUT-FREE

PREP TIME: 15 minutes / **COOK TIME:** 40 minutes

SERVES 4

Bacon seems a distinctly American addition, but it isn't very different from Chashu Pork Belly. The combination of smoky, meaty bacon and earthy Brussels sprouts makes an ideal ramen topping.

1 pound Brussels sprouts, trimmed and halved (or quartered if large)

2 tablespoons extra-virgin olive oil

½ teaspoon kosher salt

½ teaspoon freshly ground black pepper

8 ounces bacon

8 ounces fresh shiitake mushrooms, sliced

½ cup Spicy Miso Tare (page 31)

8 cups Tonkotsu (page 21)

18 ounces Basic Ramen Noodles (page 43 or store-bought) or 12 ounces dried ramen noodles

1. Preheat the oven to 425°F.

2. In a large baking dish, toss the sprouts with the olive oil, salt, and pepper. Roast until tender and browned at the edges, about 25 minutes.

3. While the sprouts are roasting, cook the bacon over medium-high heat in a large skillet until crisp, 7 to 9 minutes. Transfer the cooked bacon to a paper towel–lined plate to drain. Remove all but about 1 tablespoon of the bacon grease from the skillet.

4. In the same skillet, cook the mushrooms in the bacon grease over medium-high heat, until softened and beginning to brown, about 5 minutes. Remove from the heat.

5. Spoon 2 tablespoons of the tare into each of 4 serving bowls.

6. In a large saucepan, heat the Tonkotsu over high heat until you see bubbles around the edges and it is just about to boil.

7. Cook the noodles according to the recipe (or package instructions) and then drain well.

8. When the noodles are finished cooking, immediately ladle the hot broth into the serving bowls over the tare. Add ¼ of the noodles to each bowl. Stir gently and lift with chopsticks to distribute the tare into the broth and to coat the noodles. The noodles should float on top somewhat.

9. Top each bowl with ¼ of the Brussels sprouts and ¼ of the mushrooms. Crumble equal amounts of the bacon over the top of the bowls. Serve immediately.

MISO RAMEN WITH ROASTED TOMATO, BACON, AND EGG

DAIRY-FREE, NUT-FREE

PREP TIME: 15 minutes / **COOK TIME:** 20 minutes

SERVES 4

We love Ivan Orkin's Roasted Tomatoes ramen topper so much that we just had to create this "Americanized" bowl that pairs the tomatoes with crispy bacon and a dreamy Soft-Boiled Egg. If you are ever tempted to have a bowl of ramen for breakfast, this could be the one to choose.

8 ounces bacon

½ cup Miso Tare (page 30)

8 cups "Creamy" Chicken Broth (page 19)

18 ounces Basic Ramen Noodles (page 43 or store-bought) or 12 ounces dried ramen noodles

8 halves Roasted Tomatoes (page 61)

2 Soft-Boiled Eggs (page 55), halved lengthwise

¼ cup sliced scallions, green and white parts

1. In a large skillet, cook the bacon over medium-high heat until crisp, 7 to 9 minutes. Transfer the cooked bacon to a paper towel–lined plate to drain.

2. Spoon 2 tablespoons of the tare into each of 4 serving bowls.

3. In a large saucepan, heat the "Creamy" Chicken Broth over high heat until you see bubbles around the edges and it is just about to boil.

4. Cook the noodles according to the recipe (or package instructions) and then drain well.

5. When the noodles are finished cooking, immediately ladle the hot broth into the serving bowls over the tare. Add ¼ of the noodles to each bowl. Stir gently and lift with chopsticks to distribute the tare into the broth and to coat the noodles. The noodles should float on top somewhat.

6. Top each bowl with 2 roasted tomato halves, half of 1 Soft-Boiled Egg, and 1 tablespoon of the scallions. Crumble equal amounts of the bacon over the top of the bowls. Serve immediately.

MISO RAMEN WITH SHAVED ASPARAGUS, SCALLIONS, AND LEMON ZEST

DAIRY-FREE, NUT-FREE, VEGAN

PREP TIME: 15 minutes / **COOK TIME:** 10 minutes

SERVES 4

This vegan ramen is so delightfully simple. Earthy Shiitake Dashi and savory Miso Tare make up the base, while lightly blanched asparagus and a shower of freshly grated lemon zest make it taste like sunshine in a bowl.

Pinch salt

1 pound asparagus, woody ends snapped off

½ cup Miso Tare (page 30)

8 cups Shiitake Dashi (page 26)

18 ounces Basic Ramen Noodles (page 43 or store-bought) or 12 ounces dried ramen noodles

¼ cup sliced scallions, green and white parts

1 lemon, scrubbed

1. Prepare an ice water bath by filling a medium bowl with cold water and ice.

2. Bring a stockpot of lightly salted water to a boil over high heat. Add the asparagus and cook just 1 to 2 minutes, just until slightly softened. Use a slotted spoon to remove the asparagus from the stockpot and immediately plunge it into the ice bath to stop the cooking.

3. Use a vegetable peeler to shave the asparagus into long, thin strips.

4. Spoon 2 tablespoons of the tare into each of 4 serving bowls.

5. In a large saucepan, heat the Shiitake Dashi over high heat until you see bubbles around the edges and it is just about to boil.

6. Cook the noodles according to the recipe (or package instructions) and then drain well. When the noodles are finished cooking, immediately ladle the hot broth into the serving bowls over the tare. Add ¼ of the noodles to each bowl. Stir gently and lift with chopsticks to distribute the tare into the broth and to coat the noodles. The noodles should float on top somewhat.

7. Top each bowl with ¼ of the asparagus strips and 1 tablespoon of the scallions. Use a Microplane or grater to zest the lemon directly over the bowls of ramen. Serve immediately.

Ingredient Tip: *Choose an organic lemon, if possible, and be sure to scrub it well since you're using the zest rather than the fruit inside.*

MISO RAMEN WITH KIMCHI, SHIITAKE MUSHROOMS, AND SOY SAUCE EGGS

DAIRY-FREE, NUT-FREE, VEGETARIAN

PREP TIME: 15 minutes / **COOK TIME:** 10 minutes

SERVES 4

Kimchi—Korean fermented cabbage—brings layers of flavor to ramen: bright tartness, a hint of sweetness, funkiness from the fermentation, and a wallop of spice. For a vegan bowl, leave out the eggs, or replace them with tofu or tempeh.

½ cup Miso Tare (page 30)

8 cups Shiitake Dashi (page 26)

1 tablespoon sesame oil

8 ounces fresh shiitake mushrooms, sliced

¼ teaspoon kosher salt

18 ounces Basic Ramen Noodles (page 43 or store-bought) or 12 ounces dried ramen noodles

1 cup kimchi

2 Soy Sauce Eggs (page 56), halved lengthwise

¼ cup sliced scallions, green and white parts

1. Spoon 2 tablespoons of the tare into each of 4 serving bowls.

2. In a large saucepan, heat the Shiitake Dashi over high heat until you see bubbles around the edges and it is just about to boil.

3. While the broth is heating, heat the sesame oil in a large skillet over medium-high heat. Add the mushrooms and salt and cook, stirring occasionally, until softened and beginning to brown, about 5 minutes. Remove the pan from the heat. Set aside.

4. Cook the noodles according to the recipe (or package instructions) and then drain well.

5. When the noodles are finished cooking, immediately ladle the hot broth into the serving bowls over the tare. Add ¼ of the noodles to each bowl. Stir gently and lift with chopsticks to distribute the tare into the broth and to coat the noodles. The noodles should float on top somewhat.

6. Top each bowl with ¼ of the mushrooms, ¼ cup of the kimchi, half of 1 Soy Sauce Egg, and 1 tablespoon of the scallions. Serve immediately.

Ingredient Tip: *Most Asian markets and some grocery stores will carry kimchi.*

SPICY MISO RAMEN WITH CORN, BUTTER, SPINACH, AND SOY SAUCE EGGS

NUT-FREE, VEGETARIAN

PREP TIME: 15 minutes / **COOK TIME:** 10 minutes

SERVES 4

This colorful vegetarian ramen packs lots of flavor. The Spicy Miso Tare gives it a kick of spice and a rich, savory base. Fresh corn kernels sautéed in butter add crunch and sweetness, and a pat of butter lends the bowl added body.

½ cup Spicy Miso Tare (page 31)

8 cups Awase Dashi (page 25)

4 cups fresh spinach

¼ cup, plus 1 tablespoon butter, divided

1 cup fresh corn kernels (from 2 ears of corn)

18 ounces Basic Ramen Noodles (page 43 or store-bought) or 12 ounces dried ramen noodles

2 Soy Sauce Eggs (page 56), halved lengthwise

¼ cup sliced scallions, green and white parts

1. Spoon 2 tablespoons of the tare into each of 4 serving bowls.

2. In a large saucepan, heat the Awase Dashi over high heat until you see bubbles around the edges and it is just about to boil. Add the spinach to the broth and let it cook for a minute or so, until it wilts, then remove it with a slotted spoon.

3. While the broth is heating, heat 1 tablespoon of the butter in a medium skillet over medium-high heat. When the butter is melted and bubbling, add the corn kernels and cook, stirring frequently, for about 2 minutes, until the edges just begin to brown.

4. Cook the noodles according to the recipe (or package instructions) and then drain well.

5. When the noodles are finished cooking, immediately ladle the hot broth into the serving bowls over the tare. Add ¼ of the noodles to each bowl. Stir gently and lift with chopsticks to distribute the tare into the broth and to coat the noodles. The noodles should float on top somewhat.

6. Top each bowl with ¼ of the spinach, ¼ cup of the corn, half of 1 Soy Sauce Egg, 1 tablespoon of scallions, and a generous pat of butter. Serve immediately.

Substitution Tip: *Make this vegan by omitting the eggs (you can substitute tofu or tempeh), cooking the corn in sesame oil, and using Scallion Oil (page 40) in place of the butter on top.*

MISO RAMEN WITH SMOKY EGGPLANT, GINGER, AND SPINACH

DAIRY-FREE, NUT-FREE, VEGETARIAN

PREP TIME: 15 minutes / **COOK TIME:** 15 minutes

SERVES 4

Grilling eggplant until its skin chars and blackens gives it a delicious smoky flavor, which makes it an excellent topping for a bowl of vegetarian ramen, especially when punched up with fresh ginger.

1 eggplant or 2 Japanese eggplants

½ teaspoon kosher salt

½ cup Miso Tare (page 30)

8 cups Shiitake Dashi (page 26)

4 cups fresh spinach

18 ounces Basic Ramen Noodles (page 43 or store-bought) or 12 ounces dried ramen noodles

2 Soy Sauce Eggs (page 56), halved lengthwise

1 (2-inch) piece fresh ginger, peeled and cut into very thin matchsticks

1. Preheat a grill to high heat. Grill the eggplant a few inches from the heat, turning occasionally, until the flesh is very soft and the skin is charred and blackened in parts, about 10 minutes. Remove from the heat and let rest for a few minutes before peeling off the skin (or cut in half and scoop out the flesh). Sprinkle the flesh with salt.

2. Spoon 2 tablespoons of the tare into each of 4 serving bowls.

3. In a large saucepan, heat the Shiitake Dashi over high heat until you see bubbles around the edges and it is just about to boil. Add the spinach to the broth and let it cook for a minute or so, until it wilts, then remove it with a slotted spoon.

4. Cook the noodles according to the recipe (or package instructions) and then drain well.

5. When the noodles are finished cooking, immediately ladle the hot broth into the serving bowls over the tare. Add ¼ of the noodles to each bowl. Stir gently and lift with chopsticks to distribute the tare into the broth and to coat the noodles. The noodles should float on top somewhat.

6. Top each bowl with ¼ of the eggplant, ¼ of the spinach, half of 1 Soy Sauce Egg, and ¼ of the ginger. Serve immediately.

Ingredient Tip: *If you don't have a grill, cook the eggplant directly over the flame on a gas cooktop or under the broiler.*

SOY MILK MISO RAMEN WITH YUBA, SHIITAKE MUSHROOMS, AND PICKLED GINGER

DAIRY-FREE, NUT-FREE, VEGAN

PREP TIME: 15 minutes / **COOK TIME:** 1 hour 15 minutes

SERVES 4

Soymilk ramen broth is a Kyoto invention created by native chef Minoru Yonegawa. He simmers a rich katsuo dashi (bonito stock) with soymilk until it is silky smooth, thick, and rich. Here, we combine Shiitake Dashi with soymilk as the base for this vegan Kyoto-style bowl.

5 cups Shiitake Dashi (page 26)

5 cups soy milk

½ cup Miso Tare (page 30)

1 tablespoon sesame oil

8 ounces fresh shiitake mushrooms, sliced

¼ teaspoon kosher salt

18 ounces Basic Ramen
   Noodles (page 43 or
   store-bought) or 12 ounces
   dried ramen noodles

4 ounces yuba, cut into strips

¼ cup Red Pickled Ginger
   (page 58)

1. In a large saucepan, combine the Shiitake Dashi and soy milk and bring to a boil over high heat. Reduce the heat to medium and simmer, uncovered, until the broth thickens and is reduced by about one-third, about 1 hour.

2. Spoon 2 tablespoons of the tare into each of 4 serving bowls.

3. While the broth is heating, heat the sesame oil in a large skillet over medium-high heat. Add the mushrooms and salt and cook, stirring occasionally, until softened and beginning to brown, about 5 minutes. Remove the pan from the heat.

4. Cook the noodles according to the recipe (or package instructions) and then drain well.

5. When the noodles are finished cooking, immediately ladle the hot broth into the serving bowls over the tare. Add ¼ of the noodles to each bowl. Stir gently and lift with chopsticks to distribute the tare into the broth and to coat the noodles. The noodles should float on top somewhat.

6. Top each bowl with ¼ of the yuba, ¼ of the mushrooms, and 1 tablespoon of the Red Pickled Ginger. Serve immediately.

Ingredient Tip: *Yuba is the skin that forms when soy milk is boiled in the process of making tofu. As the soy milk boils, this film is skimmed off, dried, and cut into strips for use in cooking. Find yuba in Asian markets and some supermarkets, too.*

MISO RAMEN WITH PAN-FRIED TOFU, KABOCHA SQUASH, AND BABY BOK CHOY

DAIRY-FREE, NUT-FREE, VEGAN

PREP TIME: 15 minutes / **COOK TIME:** 1 hour

SERVES 4

In this deeply satisfying vegan ramen bowl, pan-fried tofu and baby bok choy complement the sweet kabocha squash.

8 cups Shiitake Dashi (page 26)

8 to 12 baby bok choy

1 tablespoon neutral-flavored vegetable oil

¾ cup firm tofu, cut into small rectangles

Kosher salt

½ cup Miso Tare (page 30)

18 ounces Basic Ramen Noodles (page 43 or store-bought) or 12 ounces dried ramen noodles

Roasted Kabocha Squash (page 60)

¼ cup sliced scallions, green and white parts

1 tablespoon toasted sesame seeds

1. In a large saucepan, heat the Shiitake Dashi over high heat until it is just about to boil. Stir in the baby bok choy and simmer for about 2 minutes to wilt it. Remove the pot from the heat and use a slotted spoon to remove the bok choy.

2. In a medium nonstick skillet, heat the oil over medium-high heat until it shimmers. Add the tofu, seasoning liberally with salt, and cook, stirring frequently, until nicely browned, about 5 minutes.

3. Spoon 2 tablespoons of the tare into each of 4 serving bowls.

4. Cook the noodles according to the recipe (or package instructions) and then drain well.

5. When the noodles are finished cooking, immediately ladle the hot broth into the serving bowls over the tare. Add ¼ of the noodles to each bowl. Stir gently and lift with chopsticks to distribute the tare into the broth and to coat the noodles. The noodles should float on top somewhat.

6. Top each bowl with ¼ of the squash, ¼ of the tofu, 2 or 3 baby bok choy, 1 tablespoon of scallions, and a sprinkle of sesame seeds. Serve immediately.

Substitution Tip: *If you can't find baby bok choy, you can substitute fresh spinach, kale, or Swiss chard.*

THAI-STYLE GREEN CURRY RAMEN WITH GRILLED
STEAK, SQUASH, AND GREENS, PAGE 167

OTHER RAMEN

TOKYO-STYLE TSUKEMEN

DAIRY-FREE, NUT-FREE

PREP TIME: 15 minutes / **COOK TIME:** 30 minutes

SERVES 4

Tsukemen is a style in which the noodles are served cold or at room temperature, separately from the piping-hot broth, which is used as a salty, rich dipping sauce. According to ramen lore, in 1961, the staff at a legendary Tokyo ramen shop, Higashi-Ikubukuro Taishouken, began eating their ramen this way on their lunch breaks, and the owner and ramen master Kazuo Yamagishi decided to put it on the menu. Over the ensuing decades, the style spread throughout Japan.

18 ounces Basic Ramen Noodles (page 43 or store-bought) or 12 ounces dried ramen noodles

2 tablespoons neutral-flavored vegetable oil, divided

2 garlic cloves, minced

2 tablespoons chopped fresh ginger

2 shallots, minced

8 cups Tonkotsu (page 21)

½ cup Shoyu Tare (page 32)

12 slices Chashu Pork Belly (page 49)

¼ cup sliced scallions, green and white parts

2 tablespoons sesame seeds

4 ounces enoki mushrooms

2 Soft-Boiled Eggs (page 55), halved lengthwise

1. Cook the noodles according to the recipe (or package instructions), drain, and rinse them under cold water, shaking the colander, to cool the noodles down.

2. In a large saucepan, heat 1 tablespoon of the oil over medium-high heat until it shimmers. Add the garlic, ginger, and shallots and cook, stirring frequently, until the shallot softens, about 5 minutes. Add the Tonkotsu and bring just to a boil. Reduce the heat and stir in the Shoyu Tare. Simmer, uncovered, for about 20 minutes, letting the broth reduce.

3. Meanwhile, heat the remaining tablespoon of vegetable oil in a skillet and warm the pork slices in it for 1 to 2 minutes on each side.

4. Divide the broth into 4 bowls and top with the scallions and sesame seeds, dividing equally.

5. Divide the noodles into 4 more separate bowls and top each with 3 slices of the pork, ¼ of the mushrooms, and half of 1 Soft-Boiled Egg. Serve immediately. Each diner gets a bowl of broth and a bowl of noodles, and should use the broth as a dipping sauce.

Prep-Ahead Tip: *Since the noodles are usually served cold, cook them up to a day ahead and store them, covered, in the refrigerator.*

HIROSHIMA-STYLE TSUKEMEN

DAIRY-FREE, NUT-FREE

PREP TIME: 15 minutes / **COOK TIME:** 30 minutes

SERVES 4

As it is elsewhere in the country, Hiroshima-Style Tsukemen is a dish of cold dipping noodles, but the dipping sauce is hot and spicy with a double punch of Chili Oil and chili flakes.

8 cups Pork and Chicken Broth (page 23)

1 tablespoon neutral-flavored vegetable oil

12 slices Chashu Pork Belly (page 49)

½ cup Shoyu Tare (page 32)

4 to 8 teaspoons Chili Oil (page 39)

18 ounces Basic Ramen Noodles (page 43 or store-bought) or 12 ounces dried ramen noodles

2 Soft-Boiled Eggs (page 55), halved lengthwise

12 slices cucumber

1 cup shredded cabbage

¼ cup chopped scallions, green and white parts

Dried red chili flakes, for serving

1. In a large saucepan, heat the Pork and Chicken Broth over medium-high heat and bring almost to a boil. Reduce the heat to medium and simmer, uncovered, for about 20 minutes, allowing the broth to reduce.

2. While the broth is heating, heat the vegetable oil in a skillet and warm the pork slices in it for 1 to 2 minutes on each side.

3. Spoon 2 tablespoons of the tare into each of 4 serving bowls. Add 1 to 2 teaspoons of Chili Oil to each bowl, depending on the diner's spice level preference.

4. Cook the noodles according to the recipe (or package instructions), drain, and rinse in cold running water. Chill in the refrigerator for 1 hour if desired, or serve at room temperature.

5. Ladle the hot soup into the bowls with the tare and oil and stir to mix.

6. Divide the noodles among 4 more separate bowls and top each with 3 slices of pork, half of 1 Soft-Boiled Egg, 3 cucumber slices, ¼ cup of cabbage, and 1 tablespoon of scallions. Serve immediately, passing dried chili flakes at the table. Each diner gets a bowl of broth and a bowl of noodles, and should use the broth as a dipping sauce.

Prep-Ahead Tip: *Every element of this ramen can be made a day or two in advance, if not longer. When you're ready to serve, just heat up the reduced broth and warm the Chashu Pork Belly slices.*

VEGETARIAN CURRY RAMEN WITH CARROTS, PEAS, AND SOFT-BOILED EGGS

DAIRY-FREE, NUT-FREE, VEGETARIAN

PREP TIME: 15 minutes / **COOK TIME:** 20 minutes

SERVES 4

Curry is popular in Japan. The curries there tend to be a bit sweeter and milder than what you may find in other Asian cuisines, like Indian or Thai. The ingredients list for this vegetarian curry ramen may seem a bit long, but most of the ingredients are pantry staples.

2 garlic cloves, peeled

1 (2-inch) piece peeled fresh ginger

1 shallot

1 tablespoon brown sugar

1 tablespoon curry powder

1 teaspoon ground coriander

½ teaspoon ground turmeric

1 tablespoon chili garlic paste

¼ teaspoon kosher salt

2 tablespoons neutral-flavored vegetable oil, divided

8 cups Shiitake Dashi (page 26)

1 tablespoon soy sauce

2 carrots, diced

1 cup fresh or frozen peas

18 ounces Basic Ramen Noodles (page 43 or store-bought) or 12 ounces dried ramen noodles

2 Soft-Boiled Eggs (page 55), halved lengthwise

1 sheet nori, cut into 3-inch strips

4 radishes, thinly sliced

¼ cup chopped fresh cilantro

1. In a food processor, combine the garlic, ginger, shallot, brown sugar, curry powder, coriander, turmeric, chili garlic paste, and salt and process to a smooth purée.

2. In a large saucepan, heat 1 tablespoon of the oil over medium-high heat until it shimmers. Add the curry mixture and cook, stirring, for 1 minute. Add the Shiitake Dashi and reduce the heat to medium. Bring almost to a boil, then stir in the soy sauce.

3. In a small skillet, heat the remaining tablespoon of oil over medium-high heat until it shimmers. Add the carrots and cook, stirring frequently, until softened, about 5 minutes. Add the peas and cook, stirring, until just heated through, about 2 minutes more. Remove the pan from the heat.

4. Cook the noodles according to the recipe (or package instructions) and then drain well.

5. When the noodles are finished cooking, immediately ladle the hot broth into the serving bowls. Add ¼ of the noodles to each bowl and then lift the noodles up with chopsticks and gently lay them back into the broth, letting them float on top somewhat. Top each bowl with half of 1 Soft-Boiled Egg, ¼ of the peas and carrots mixture, ¼ of the nori strips, ¼ of the radishes, and 1 tablespoon of the cilantro. Serve immediately.

Substitution Tip: *Save time on this recipe by using a ready-made Japanese-style curry sauce mix. Skip step 1 of the cooking instructions and replace the homemade curry paste with the sauce mix in step 2.*

THAI-STYLE GREEN CURRY RAMEN WITH GRILLED STEAK, SQUASH, AND GREENS

DAIRY-FREE, NUT-FREE

PREP TIME: 15 minutes / **COOK TIME:** 20 minutes

SERVES 4

Indian and Japanese curries rely on dried, ground spices for their flavor. Thai curries, on the other hand, usually start with a curry paste made by grinding fresh chiles, spices, and aromatics together. Although this broth is often quite spicy, coconut milk helps cool things down, while also adding body and richness. Serving this curry ramen-style—filled with tender noodles and topped with meat and veggies—makes perfect sense.

2 tablespoons neutral-flavored vegetable oil

2 garlic cloves, minced

1 tablespoon minced fresh ginger

1 to 3 tablespoons Thai green curry paste

1 tablespoon brown sugar

6½ cups Clear Chicken Broth (page 17)

4 cups fresh spinach

1 (15-ounce) can coconut milk

1 tablespoon fish sauce

1 pound top sirloin steak, about ½-inch thick

Kosher salt

Freshly ground black pepper

2 cups diced kabocha squash

18 ounces Basic Ramen Noodles (page 43 or store-bought) or 12 ounces dried ramen noodles

¼ cup chopped fresh cilantro

1 lime, cut into wedges, for garnish

1. In a stockpot, heat the oil over medium heat. Add the garlic, ginger, and Thai green curry paste and cook, stirring, for 2 minutes. Add the brown sugar and cook, stirring, for 1 minute more. Add the Clear Chicken Broth and raise the heat to medium-high. Bring almost to a boil. Add the spinach and cook for 1 to 2 minutes, until just wilted. Use a slotted spoon to remove the spinach from the broth.

2. Stir the coconut milk and fish sauce into the broth and heat until it comes back up to almost boiling.

3. Preheat the grill to medium-high heat. Season the steak generously with salt and pepper and grill for about 3 minutes per side for medium-rare. Remove from the heat and let rest for at least 5 minutes before slicing against the grain into ¼-inch-thick slices.

4. Place the squash in a medium microwave-safe bowl and add ⅓ cup water. Cover and heat in the microwave for 3 to 5 minutes, until the squash is tender. Drain.

5. Cook the noodles according to the recipe (or package instructions) and then drain well.

6. When the noodles are finished cooking, immediately ladle the hot broth into the serving bowls. Add ¼ of the noodles to each bowl and then lift the noodles up with chopsticks and gently lay them back into the broth, letting them float on top somewhat.

Continued

7. Top each bowl with ¼ of the steak, ¼ of the squash, ¼ of the spinach, and 1 tablespoon of the cilantro. Serve immediately with a wedge of lime for diners to squeeze into the soup as desired.

Ingredient Tip: You can find Thai-style curry paste in Asian markets and in most supermarkets. As they vary wildly in terms of spiciness level, start with 1 tablespoon and adjust to your liking.

SPICY LAKSA RAMEN WITH RED CURRY, FRIED TOFU PUFFS, AND GREEN BEANS

DAIRY-FREE, NUT-FREE, VEGAN

PREP TIME: 15 minutes / **COOK TIME:** 20 minutes

SERVES 4

Laksa is a Malaysian spicy noodle soup. As with ramen, there are many different recipes, but the most common in the United States features a rich, coconut milk–enriched broth, red chiles, and a base of curry paste. Rice noodles are used in a classic laksa; feel free to substitute them here for a gluten-free version (remember to use gluten-free soy sauce, too).

2 tablespoons neutral-flavored vegetable oil

2 garlic cloves, minced

1 tablespoon minced fresh ginger

1 lemongrass stalk, white part only, finely minced

2 to 4 tablespoons red curry paste (see Ingredient Tip)

1 tablespoon brown sugar

6½ cups Shiitake Dashi (page 26)

1 (15-ounce) can coconut milk

1 tablespoon soy sauce

18 ounces Basic Ramen Noodles (page 43 or store-bought) or 12 ounces dried ramen noodles

3 ounces fried tofu puffs, halved (see Ingredient Tip)

8 ounces green beans, cut into 2-inch pieces and steamed until crisp-tender

½ cup bean sprouts

¼ cup cilantro

1 lime, cut into wedges, for garnish

1. In a stockpot, heat the oil over medium heat. Add the garlic, ginger, lemongrass, and red curry paste and cook, stirring, for 2 minutes. Add the brown sugar and cook, stirring, for 1 minute more. Add the Awase Dashi and raise the heat to medium-high. Bring almost to a boil. Stir the coconut milk and soy sauce into the broth and heat until it comes back up to almost boiling.

2. Cook the noodles according to the recipe (or package instructions) and then drain well.

3. When the noodles are finished cooking, immediately ladle the hot broth into 4 serving bowls. Add ¼ of the noodles to each bowl and then lift the noodles up with the chopsticks and gently lay them back into the broth, letting them float on top somewhat. Top each bowl with ¼ of the tofu puffs, ¼ of the green beans, ¼ of the bean sprouts, and 1 tablespoon of the cilantro. Serve immediately with a wedge of lime for diners to squeeze into the soup as desired.

Ingredient Tip: *Malaysian laksa paste can be found in Asian markets, but it usually has dried shrimp and other seafood-based ingredients in it. Store-bought Indian or Thai red curry pastes are often vegan (but always check the ingredients to be sure). Fried tofu puffs can also be found in Asian markets.*

RAMEN SALAD (*HIYASHI CHUKA*)

DAIRY-FREE, NUT-FREE

PREP TIME: 15 minutes / **COOK TIME:** 5 minutes

SERVES 4

This chilled ramen is tossed in a light vinaigrette made with rice wine vinegar and Japanese hot mustard. It is super refreshing—the perfect way to eat ramen on a hot day. Make it your own by experimenting with cooked shrimp, sliced Chashu Pork Belly, edamame, or shredded lettuce.

FOR THE NOODLES

18 ounces Basic Ramen
  Noodles (page 43 or
  store-bought) or 12 ounces
  dried ramen noodles

FOR THE DRESSING

¼ cup rice wine vinegar

¼ cup soy sauce

2 tablespoons sugar

1 tablespoon Japanese hot
  mustard

2 tablespoons toasted
  sesame oil

2 tablespoons neutral-flavored
  vegetable oil

FOR THE SALAD

2 eggs, beaten

1 Kirby or Persian cucumber,
  cut into matchsticks

⅓ cup thick-cut ham, cut into
  strips

10 grape tomatoes, halved

1½ tablespoons toasted
  sesame seeds

1 scallion, chopped

TO MAKE THE NOODLES

Cook the noodles according to the recipe (or package instructions), drain, and immediately rinse well under cold running water to cool. If prepping ahead, refrigerate, covered, until ready to use.

TO MAKE THE DRESSING

In a medium bowl, whisk together the rice wine vinegar, soy sauce, sugar, and Japanese hot mustard. Add the sesame oil and vegetable oil and whisk to combine well.

TO MAKE THE SALAD

1. Heat a medium nonstick skillet over medium heat. Coat the pan with a bit of vegetable oil and add the eggs. Cook until set into a thin, flat omelet. Slide the eggs out of the pan and onto a plate and let cool. Slice into strips.

2. Assemble the salad by plating the noodles on a wide dish or bowl and topping it with the cucumber, ham, tomato, and egg strips.

3. Toss the dressing with the salad and sprinkle the sesame seeds and scallions on top. Serve immediately or refrigerate until ready to serve.

Substitution Tip: *Make this salad vegan by omitting the egg and ham. Add tofu, tempeh, or edamame for added protein if you like.*

HIROSHIMA-STYLE TANTANMEN

DAIRY-FREE, NUT-FREE

PREP TIME: 5 minutes / **COOK TIME:** 20 minutes

SERVES 4

Tantanmen (see our Tonkotsu-based version on page 91) is a Japanese interpretation of spicy Chinese dan dan noodles. In Hiroshima, the noodles are served naked, with a spicy, meaty dipping sauce and spices on the side. The trick is to swirl the noodles in the sauce until fully coated—then season.

1 tablespoon sesame oil

1 tablespoon doubanjiang

1 garlic clove, minced

1½ teaspoons grated ginger

1 scallion, sliced

½ pound ground pork

¼ cup soy sauce

1 tablespoon sake

1 tablespoon white miso paste

2 tablespoons Japanese
sesame paste

1 cup water

1 teaspoon Chili Oil (page 39)

18 ounces Basic Ramen
Noodles (page 43 or
store-bought) or 12 ounces
dried ramen noodles

Sichuan peppercorns, for
serving (optional)

1. In a medium skillet, heat the sesame oil over medium-high heat until it shimmers. Add the doubanjiang, garlic, ginger, and scallion and cook, stirring, for 30 seconds. Add the pork and cook, stirring frequently, for 3 minutes.

2. Stir in the soy sauce, sake, white miso, and Japanese sesame paste. Add the water and bring to a boil. Reduce the heat to low, stir in the Chili Oil, and simmer for 5 minutes.

3. Cook the noodles according to the recipe (or package instructions) and then drain well.

4. Divide the noodles among 4 serving bowls. Serve the sauce alongside the noodles. Pass Sichuan peppercorns at the table, if desired.

Substitution Tip: *To make this dish vegan, omit the pork and substitute crumbled firm tofu.*

PINEAPPLE RAMEN WITH HAM, NORI, CHILE THREADS, AND PINEAPPLE-CURED EGGS

DAIRY-FREE, NUT-FREE

PREP TIME: 15 minutes, plus 2 hours to marinate / **COOK TIME:** 20 minutes

SERVES 4

Whether pineapple belongs in savory dishes sparks many debates. If you're on the pro side, you'll love that a pineapple-themed Tokyo ramen-ya exists—every dish contains pineapple. Here, the sweet, tart, and juicy fruit partners well with savory, rich ingredients like ham and Tonkotsu. If you weren't previously on the pro side, this may convert you.

2 Soft-Boiled Eggs (page 55), peeled

2 cups pineapple juice, divided

½ cup Shio Tare (page 33)

7 cups Tonkotsu (page 21)

½ pound diced cooked ham

18 ounces Basic Ramen Noodles (page 43 or store-bought) or 12 ounces dried ramen noodles

1 cup diced fresh pineapple

1 sheet nori, cut into 3-inch strips

2 tablespoons chile threads

1. Combine the eggs and ⅔ cup of the pineapple juice in a bowl or jar. Cover and refrigerate for at least 2 hours.

2. Spoon 2 tablespoons of the tare into each of 4 serving bowls.

3. In a large saucepan, heat the Tonkotsu over high heat until you see bubbles around the edges and it is just about to boil. Stir in the remaining 1⅓ cups pineapple juice and let the mixture return to a simmer. Remove from the heat.

4. Meanwhile, heat a large skillet over medium-high heat. Add the ham and cook, stirring occasionally, for 3 to 4 minutes, until lightly browned. Remove the pan from the heat.

5. Cook the noodles according to the recipe (or package instructions) and then drain well.

6. When the noodles are finished cooking, immediately ladle the hot broth into the serving bowls over the tare. Add ¼ of the noodles to each bowl. Stir gently and lift with chopsticks to distribute the tare into the broth and to coat the noodles. The noodles should float on top somewhat.

7. Top each bowl with ¼ of the ham, ¼ cup of the pineapple, ¼ of
    the nori, and ½ tablespoon of chile threads. Slice the Soft-Boiled
    Eggs in half, lengthwise, and add one half to each bowl. Serve
    immediately.

~~~~~~

Ingredient Tip: *Chile threads are thinly sliced dried Korean red
peppers with a slightly fruity, sweet, and mildly spicy flavor. They
can be found in the spice section of Japanese or Korean specialty
markets and in most Asian supermarkets.*

~~~~~~

SPICY RED TONKOTSU RAMEN WITH CHICKEN, CABBAGE, AND WAKAME

DAIRY-FREE, NUT-FREE

PREP TIME: 15 minutes / **COOK TIME:** 15 minutes

SERVES 4

Tonkotsu ramen is rich and filling, just the kind of thing you want when you're feeling under the weather. Add a wallop of spicy heat from chiles and it will cure what ails you. To balance the broth's zingy spice, this bowl is topped with crunchy fresh cabbage, shredded chicken, and wakame.

½ cup Shio Tare (page 33)

4 teaspoons doubanjiang or chili garlic paste

8 cups Tonkotsu (page 21)

18 ounces Basic Ramen Noodles (page 43 or store-bought) or 12 ounces dried ramen noodles

¾ pound shredded, cooked chicken

2 Soy Sauce Eggs (page 56), sliced in half lengthwise

4 teaspoons Chili Oil (page 39)

1 cup shredded cabbage

½ cup wakame (seaweed)

1. Spoon 2 tablespoons of the tare into each of 4 serving bowls. Add 1 teaspoon doubanjiang to each bowl.

2. In a large saucepan, heat the Tonkotsu over high heat until you see bubbles around the edges and it is just about to boil.

3. Cook the noodles according to the recipe (or package instructions) and then drain well.

4. When the noodles are finished cooking, immediately ladle the hot broth into the serving bowls over the tare and doubanjiang. Add ¼ of the noodles to each bowl. Stir gently and lift with chopsticks to distribute the tare into the broth and to coat the noodles. The noodles should float on top somewhat.

5. Top each bowl with ¼ of the chicken, half of 1 Soy Sauce Egg, 1 teaspoon of Chili Oil, ¼ cup of the cabbage, and ¼ of the wakame. If you or your guests prefer more heat, pass additional Chili Oil at the table. Serve immediately.

Ingredient Tip: *Use leftover roasted chicken or purchase a rotisserie chicken.*

SPICY STIR-FRIED GARLIC RAMEN (*YAKISOBA*)

DAIRY-FREE, NUT-FREE, VEGAN

PREP TIME: 10 minutes / **COOK TIME:** 10 minutes

SERVES 4

This quick super flavorful dish is the kind of thing you see in street food stalls and at festivals in Japan, often served along with cabbage, bean sprouts, onions, carrots, and tofu or shrimp.

18 ounces Basic Ramen Noodles (page 43 or store-bought) or 12 ounces dried ramen noodles

1 tablespoon neutral-flavored vegetable oil

1 teaspoon sesame oil

2 garlic cloves, minced

⅓ cup low-sodium soy sauce

2 teaspoons brown sugar

2 tablespoons chili paste or gochujang

1 tablespoon toasted sesame seeds

1 scallion, thinly sliced

1. Cook the noodles until al dente and then drain well.

2. In a large skillet, heat the vegetable oil and sesame oil over medium heat until it shimmers.

3. Add the garlic and cook, stirring, for 1 minute. Remove the pan from the heat.

4. Whisk in the soy sauce, brown sugar, and chili paste.

5. Toss the noodles with the sauce and serve garnished with toasted sesame seeds and scallions.

Repurposing Tip: *Store these noodles, covered, in the refrigerator for up to 3 days. To serve them cold, you can add shredded cabbage or lettuce and diced cucumbers for added crunch.*

SPICY PEANUT RAMEN

DAIRY-FREE, VEGAN

PREP TIME: 10 minutes / **COOK TIME:** 20 minutes
SERVES 4

I love this quick vegan ramen because it uses ingredients that I almost always have on hand. Tasty potential additions include mushrooms, sautéed greens, diced fresh radishes, or fresh microgreens. If you've got fresh herbs like basil or mint, go ahead and add those along with the cilantro.

1 tablespoon neutral-flavored vegetable oil

3 garlic cloves, minced

1 tablespoon minced fresh ginger

1 tablespoon chili paste

5 cups Shiitake Dashi (page 26)

1 (14-ounce) can coconut milk

½ cup no-sugar-added, smooth peanut butter

2 tablespoons brown sugar

18 ounces Basic Ramen Noodles (page 43 or store-bought) or 12 ounces dried ramen noodles

2 tablespoons soy sauce

Juice of 2 limes

1 cup diced silken tofu

¼ cup chopped fresh cilantro

¼ cup chopped roasted, unsalted peanuts

¼ cup sliced scallions, green and white parts

1. In a large saucepan, heat the vegetable oil over medium-high heat until it shimmers. Add the garlic and ginger and cook, stirring, for 1 minute. Stir in the chili paste, and then add the Shiitake Dashi and coconut milk and bring just to a boil. Reduce the heat to low, whisk in the peanut butter and brown sugar, and let simmer for 10 to 15 minutes.

2. Cook the noodles according to the recipe (or package instructions) and then drain well.

3. Stir the soy sauce and lime juice into the broth mixture.

4. To serve, ladle the broth into 4 serving bowls and then add the noodles, dividing equally. Top each bowl with ¼ cup of tofu, 1 tablespoon of the cilantro, 1 tablespoon of the peanuts, and 1 tablespoon of the scallions. Serve immediately.

Prep-Ahead Tip: *The broth for this ramen will keep for up to a week in the refrigerator.*

CHILLED DASHI RAMEN WITH SHRIMP, SOY SAUCE EGGS, AND SHISO LEAVES

DAIRY-FREE, NUT-FREE

PREP TIME: 10 minutes, plus 1 hour to chill the broth / **COOK TIME:** 10 minutes

SERVES 4

The lightness of this broth makes for a great chilled soup. If you like it so much you want to keep eating it once the weather turns, the whole dish can be served hot, too. Either way, slurping is encouraged.

2 tablespoons white miso

8 cups Awase Dashi (page 25)

18 ounces Basic Ramen Noodles (page 43 or store-bought) or 12 ounces dried ramen noodles

¾ pound cooked shrimp

4 Soy Sauce Eggs (page 56), halved lengthwise

¼ cup sliced scallions, green and white parts

4 shiso leaves, julienned

1. In a large bowl, whisk together the white miso and Awase Dashi. Cover and refrigerate for at least 1 hour.

2. Cook the noodles according to the recipe (or package instructions), drain, and immediately rinse well under cold running water to cool. If prepping ahead, refrigerate, covered, until ready to use.

3. To serve, divide the noodles among 4 serving bowls. Add ¼ of the broth to each bowl and then top with ¼ of the shrimp, 2 egg halves, 1 tablespoon of the scallions, and ¼ of the shiso leaves.

Ingredient Tip: *Shiso, also known as perilla, is a leafy herb that is usually green (though there is a red variety, as well). It is a common garnish in Japanese cooking. It has a distinctive spicy flavor, reminiscent of cinnamon and cloves, as well as other leafy green herbs like cilantro.*

SPICY PORK MAZEMEN WITH MUSTARD GREENS, POACHED EGGS, AND GARLIC

DAIRY-FREE, NUT-FREE

PREP TIME: 10 minutes / **COOK TIME:** 25 minutes

SERVES 4

Mazemen is ramen served without broth, but with a savory sauce instead. The noodles are meant to be mixed together with the sauce and toppings just before eating. In this recipe, the sauce is fortified by ground pork and chili garlic paste and given extra body with poached eggs.

1 pound ground pork

½ teaspoon salt

1 tablespoon peeled and minced fresh ginger

1½ cups Tonkotsu (page 21)

1 tablespoon chili garlic paste

1 teaspoon soy sauce

4 large eggs

18 ounces Basic Ramen Noodles (page 43 or store-bought) or 12 ounces dried ramen noodles

2 garlic cloves

1 cup sautéed mustard greens

¼ cup sliced scallions, green and white parts

1. Heat a large skillet over medium-high heat. Add the pork and salt and cook, stirring occasionally and breaking up with a spatula, until the meat is browned, about 5 minutes. Add the ginger and cook, stirring, for 1 minute more. Stir in the Tonkotsu, chili garlic paste, and soy sauce and bring to a boil. Reduce the heat to medium-low and simmer, uncovered, until the sauce thickens, 15 to 20 minutes.

2. Heat a medium saucepan of water to a simmer over high heat. Reduce the heat to low, crack the eggs into the pot, and poach for 4 minutes, until the whites are set and the yolks are still runny. Immediately remove the eggs from the water with a slotted spoon and gently transfer to a bowl.

3. Cook the noodles according to the recipe (or package instructions) and then drain well.

4. Ladle the sauce equally into 4 small bowls and grate the garlic over the tops.

5. To serve, divide the noodles among 4 serving bowls. Top each bowl with 1 poached egg, ¼ cup of mustard greens, and 1 tablespoon of scallions. Serve the sauce alongside the noodles. To eat, pour the sauce over the noodles and stir to mix well, breaking the egg yolk in the process.

CHILLED VEGAN MAZEMEN WITH SPICY TOFU AND CUCUMBER IN YUZU VINAIGRETTE

DAIRY-FREE, NUT-FREE, VEGAN

PREP TIME: 10 minutes, plus 1 hour to marinate / **COOK TIME:** 45 minutes

SERVES 4

This ramen is almost a cross between a chilled ramen salad and a classic mazemen. The noodles are served chilled, topped with fresh vegetables and baked tofu, and the "sauce" is an uncooked vinaigrette. This is a refreshing way to enjoy ramen on a warm day.

FOR THE VINAIGRETTE

¼ cup yuzu juice

¼ cup extra-virgin olive oil

2 tablespoons soy sauce

2 tablespoons mirin

FOR THE TOFU

2 tablespoons low-sodium soy sauce

2 tablespoons chili paste

2 tablespoons minced fresh ginger

2 tablespoons hoisin sauce

1 (17-ounce) package firm tofu, drained and cut into ½-inch-wide strips (see Ingredient Tip)

Vegetable spray

TO MAKE THE VINAIGRETTE

In a small bowl, whisk together the yuzu juice, olive oil, soy sauce, and mirin. Set aside.

TO MAKE THE TOFU

1. In a medium bowl, stir together the soy sauce, chili paste, ginger, and hoisin sauce. Add the tofu and toss to coat well. Cover and refrigerate for at least 1 hour or as long as overnight.

2. Preheat the oven to 375°F. Spray a large baking sheet with vegetable spray. Remove the tofu from the marinade, and arrange it in a single layer on the baking sheet. Bake for 30 to 35 minutes, flipping over about halfway through the cooking time. Remove from the oven and cool to room temperature or chill before serving.

Continued

FOR THE RAMEN

18 ounces Basic Ramen
Noodles (page 43 or
store-bought) or 12 ounces
dried ramen noodles

1 small Japanese or Persian
cucumber, sliced

¼ cup sliced scallions, green
and white parts

TO MAKE THE RAMEN

1. Cook the noodles according to the recipe (or package instructions), drain, and immediately rinse well under cold running
water to cool. If prepping ahead, refrigerate, covered, until
ready to use.

2. To serve, divide the vinaigrette among 4 small bowls. Divide the
noodles among 4 serving bowls. Top each noodle bowl with ¼ of
the tofu, ¼ of the cucumber, and 1 tablespoon of the scallions.
To eat, pour the vinaigrette over the noodles and stir to mix well.

Ingredient Tip: *Place the tofu on a paper towel–lined plate. Place
more paper towels and another plate on top of the tofu to press out
the water from the tofu. Let sit at least 5 minutes.*

FRIED SHISHITO PEPPERS, PAGE 185

SIDES

QUICK-PICKLED CUCUMBERS

DAIRY-FREE, GLUTEN-FREE, NUT-FREE, VEGAN

PREP TIME: 5 minutes, plus 4 hours to chill

MAKES ABOUT 1½ CUPS

Pickles (*tsukemono*) accompany many Japanese meals. Veggies and fruits can be pickled in salt, rice wine vinegar, miso paste, soy sauce, fermented rice bran, or leftover sake rice mash. Some tsukemono take months to prepare, but these whip up in an afternoon and are ready by dinner.

2 Japanese or Persian cucumbers, thinly sliced into rounds

1 tablespoon kosher salt

1 teaspoon toasted sesame seeds

1 (2-inch) piece kombu, rinsed

1. In a bowl, toss the cucumbers with the salt, making sure each slice is well coated. Add the sesame seeds and toss to incorporate.

2. Arrange the cucumbers so that the slices are lying flat in the bowl (they can be piled up on top of one another) and then lay the kombu on top. Place a plate on top of the kombu and weigh it down with an unopened can of beans or another heavy object. (If you have a pickle press, use that instead of a weighted plate.)

3. Refrigerate the pickles for at least 4 hours. Discard the kombu before serving. The pickles will keep in an airtight container in the refrigerator for up to 5 days.

FRIED SHISHITO PEPPERS

DAIRY-FREE, GLUTEN-FREE, NUT-FREE, VEGAN

PREP TIME: 1 minute / **COOK TIME:** 6 minutes

SERVES 4 TO 6

Shishito peppers are small green peppers, about the size of a serrano pepper. On the surface, they resemble any typical green chile, but they have a fun secret. Although generally mild in flavor—comparable with the heat level of a green bell pepper—about one in every 10 shishito is spicy hot! There is no way to tell by looking at the peppers which will have that extra kick, so eating them is a bit of an adventure.

2 tablespoons neutral-flavored vegetable oil

8 ounces shishito peppers, kept whole

Flaky sea salt (such as Maldon brand)

1. In a large, heavy skillet (ideally cast iron), heat the oil over medium heat until it shimmers. Add the peppers in a single layer. Cook, undisturbed, for 2 to 3 minutes, until the bottoms are blackened and beginning to blister. Flip the peppers and cook for 2 to 3 minutes more until the peppers are blistered and charred on the second side and have softened.

2. Transfer the peppers to a serving plate and season liberally with flaky sea salt. Serve immediately.

Substitution Tip: *For extra flavor, substitute 1 tablespoon sesame oil for 1 tablespoon of the vegetable oil.*

SPICY BEAN SPROUT SALAD

DAIRY-FREE, NUT-FREE, VEGAN

PREP TIME: 5 minutes / **COOK TIME**: 1 minute

SERVES 4 TO 6

This simple salad consists of bean sprouts in a dressing of sesame oil, soy sauce, and seasonings. The kick of spice comes from shichimi togarashi, which translates to "seven-flavor chili pepper." In Japan, this dish is often complementary and available at each table in ramen shops. Enjoy it as an appetizer or as a ramen topping.

12 ounces bean sprouts

2 tablespoons sesame oil

1½ teaspoons soy sauce

1½ teaspoons shichimi
  togarashi

½ teaspoon kosher salt

1 tablespoon toasted
  sesame seeds

Freshly ground black pepper

1. Bring a saucepan of water to a boil over high heat. Add the bean sprouts and cook for about 1 minute, just to blanch them. Drain.

2. In a medium bowl, whisk together the sesame oil, soy sauce, shichimi togarashi, and salt. Add the bean sprouts and toasted sesame seeds and toss to mix. Season with pepper. Serve immediately.

3. Stored in a covered container, this salad keeps in the refrigerator for up to 3 days.

Ingredient Tip: *Shichimi togarashi is a spice mix that contains seven seasonings, including dried red chili pepper, citrus peel, sesame seeds, sansho peppercorns, ginger, garlic, and seaweed. You'll find shichimi togarashi in the Asian foods aisle of most supermarkets and in Asian markets.*

SPINACH GOMAAE

DAIRY-FREE, VEGAN

PREP TIME: 5 minutes / **COOK TIME:** 5 minutes

SERVES 4

This simple side dish—flash-wilted spinach in a deeply sesame-scented sauce—is so easy to prepare, it's virtually impossible to get wrong. Freshly ground sesame seeds give the dressing a pronounced nuttiness. The dressing relies upon an essential Japanese proportion: one part soy sauce, one part sugar, one part ground sesame seeds.

1 pound fresh spinach

2 tablespoons toasted white sesame seeds

2 tablespoons sugar

2 tablespoons soy sauce

1. Set a medium saucepan filled with water on the stove over high heat and bring to a boil.

2. Fill a bowl with ice and water to make an ice water bath for the spinach.

3. Heat a small skillet over high heat and add the sesame seeds. Cook, shaking the pan frequently, until the seeds begin to pop and become fragrant, about 1 minute. Remove the pan from the heat and transfer the seeds immediately to a bowl to stop the cooking.

4. Grind the sesame seeds, using either a spice grinder or mortar and pestle.

5. In a small bowl, combine the ground sesame seeds, sugar, and soy sauce.

6. When the water is boiling, drop the spinach in and wait about 30 to 45 seconds, until just wilted. Remove from the water with a sieve and plunge it directly into the ice water bath to stop the cooking. Drain well. Squeeze the spinach to remove excess moisture, and cut it into 2-inch lengths.

7. Toss the spinach with the sauce and serve immediately. Gomaae can be stored, covered, in the refrigerator for up to 2 days.

Substitution Tip: *If you don't have white sesame seeds, you can substitute Japanese sesame paste, or try a mixture of 1 tablespoon smooth, no-sugar-added peanut butter and 1 teaspoon sesame oil.*

SMASHED CUCUMBER SALAD (*TATAKI KYURI*)

DAIRY-FREE, NUT-FREE, VEGAN

PREP TIME: 5 minutes

SERVES 4

Smashing the cucumbers for this recipe is fun and also serves an important purpose. By breaking the cucumbers into chunks this way—rather than cutting them with a knife—you create jagged edges and more surface area to absorb the savory dressing.

3 small, chilled Persian or Japanese cucumbers, ends trimmed off (see Ingredient Tip)

1 tablespoon soy sauce

½ teaspoon sesame oil

½ teaspoon rice wine vinegar

1 small, dried, hot red chile (any type), sliced thin (optional)

1 tablespoon toasted sesame seeds, for garnish

1. Place the cucumbers in a sturdy resealable plastic bag and press out as much air as you can before sealing the top. Place the bag on a cutting board.

2. Using a rolling pin or an empty bottle, whack several spots on each cucumber so that they break into chunks.

3. Add the soy sauce, sesame oil, rice wine vinegar, and chile (if using) to the bag and massage the mixture into the cucumbers.

4. Transfer the cucumber chunks to a serving plate and garnish with the sesame seeds. Serve immediately or refrigerate for up to 2 hours; after that point, they lose their crunch.

Ingredient Tip: *Look for small, thin-skinned Japanese or Persian cucumbers for this dish. If those aren't available, you can substitute stubbier Kirby cucumbers.*

STIR-FRIED EGGPLANT, MUSHROOMS, AND PEPPERS WITH MISO

DAIRY-FREE, VEGAN

PREP TIME: 5 minutes / **COOK TIME:** 10 minutes

SERVES 4

This easy vegetable side makes a great vegetarian filling for onigiri (Japanese rice balls) and can also be used as a topping for rice or noodles. For a more intense flavor, you can substitute red miso paste for the white.

2 tablespoons white miso paste

2 tablespoons mirin

2 tablespoons soy sauce

1 tablespoon neutral-flavored vegetable oil

1 teaspoon sesame oil

2 Japanese eggplants, thinly sliced

2 black trumpet mushrooms, thinly sliced

1 red bell pepper, seeded and chopped

1. In a small bowl, stir together the white miso paste, mirin, and soy sauce.

2. In a large skillet, heat the vegetable oil over medium-high heat until it shimmers. Add the sesame oil, eggplants, mushrooms, and pepper and cook, stirring frequently, until softened, about 5 minutes.

3. Add the miso mixture, toss to coat, and cook for 2 minutes more, until the sauce thickens and coats the vegetables.

Ingredient Tip: *Black trumpet mushrooms have a complex, smoky, and fruity flavor that partners well with this sweet-salty miso sauce. If you can't find trumpet mushrooms, substitute chanterelles, shiitakes, or even button mushrooms.*

SHRIMP TEMPURA

DAIRY-FREE

PREP TIME: 10 minutes / **COOK TIME:** 15 minutes

SERVES 4

Plump shrimp lightly battered and cooked to a golden crisp make a great appetizer or side dish to ramen. To keep oil splatters contained, use a high-sided pot filled with about 3 inches of oil.

Neutral-flavored vegetable oil, for frying

1½ cups all-purpose flour

¾ cup cornstarch

1½ tablespoons baking powder

½ teaspoon kosher salt

¼ teaspoon white pepper

1 pound tail-on shrimp, peeled and deveined

1½ cups ice water

½ cup Awase Dashi (page 25)

2 tablespoons soy sauce

2 tablespoons mirin

1. Fill a deep pot with about 3 inches of vegetable oil and heat over medium-high heat to 375°F.

2. In a large mixing bowl, whisk together the flour, cornstarch, baking powder, salt, and white pepper.

3. Dredge the shrimp lightly in the dry ingredients and put aside.

4. Whisk the water into the dry ingredients, just to combine. Dunk the dredged shrimp in the batter to coat.

5. Cook the shrimp, a few at a time so as to not crowd the pot, for 2 to 3 minutes each until golden brown.

6. In a small dipping bowl, stir together the Awase Dashi, soy sauce, and mirin.

7. Serve the shrimp immediately with the dipping sauce on the side.

Substitution Tip: *To make vegan tempura, follow the recipe above, substituting vegetables for the shrimp. Try including broccoli florets (steam for 2 minutes before dredging in the dry mix and coating in the batter), sliced sweet potato (steam for 5 minutes), or sliced onions (blanch in boiling water for 30 seconds). Shiitake Dashi (page 26) also makes a wonderful dipping sauce.*

CRISPY FRIED SQUID (*IKA FURAI*)

DAIRY-FREE, NUT-FREE

PREP TIME: 10 minutes / **COOK TIME:** 5 minutes

SERVES 4

This is essentially tempura-fried squid (*ika* in Japanese) that serves up crispy, golden-brown morsels. To enjoy, dip these into your favorite tempura dipping sauce or sweet Japanese mayonnaise.

Neutral-flavored vegetable oil, for frying

¾ cup all-purpose flour

¼ cup potato starch

1 large egg

¾ cup ice water

1 pound squid rings and tentacles

Shichimi togarashi

Kosher salt

1. Fill a deep pot with about 3 inches of vegetable oil and heat over medium-high heat to 375°F.

2. In a medium bowl, whisk together the flour and potato starch.

3. In a separate bowl, whisk together the egg and water.

4. Add the egg mixture to the dry ingredients and whisk just to combine.

5. Dunk several rings and tentacles into the batter at one time and then fry them in the hot oil for about 45 seconds, until golden brown. Remove from the oil and drain on paper towels. Repeat until all the squid has been fried.

6. Serve hot, sprinkled with shichimi togarashi and salt.

Repurposing Tip: *If you have leftover batter, make tenkasu (tempura scraps) for use in Savory Cabbage Pancakes (page 192) or Octopus Dumplings (page 194). Simply dribble the batter into the hot oil, cook until golden, and remove with a slotted spoon. Let cool to room temperature before storing in a plastic bag in the freezer.*

SAVORY CABBAGE PANCAKE (*OKONOMIYAKI*)

DAIRY-FREE, NUT-FREE

PREP TIME: 15 minutes / **COOK TIME:** 10 minutes

MAKES 4 PANCAKES

Okonomiyaki is a popular snack that originated in Osaka. It's a savory cabbage pancake made with grated Japanese yam (*nagaimo* or *yamaimo*) as a binder along with eggs. Often topped with pork, it can truly pair with almost anything: shrimp, octopus, squid, chicken, scallions, or kimchi.

FOR THE PANCAKES

1 cup all-purpose flour

¾ cup Awase Dashi
   (page 25) or dashi made from
   store-bought powder

1 (3-inch) piece Japanese yam,
   peeled and grated

¼ teaspoon kosher salt

¼ teaspoon sugar

¼ teaspoon baking powder

4 large eggs

1 pound cabbage, cut into
   2-inch pieces

1¼ cup tenkasu (tempura
   scraps, optional, page 191)

¼ cup sesame oil, divided

8 thin slices fresh pork
   belly or bacon

Japanese mayonnaise
   (optional), for serving

Bonito flakes (katsuobushi),
   for garnish

TO MAKE THE PANCAKES

1. In a large mixing bowl, combine the flour, Awase Dashi, Japanese yam, salt, sugar, and baking powder. Add the eggs and mix just until well combined. Stir in the cabbage and the tenkasu (if using).

2. Heat a large skillet over medium-high heat. Add 1 tablespoon of the sesame oil, swirling to coat the pan. Scoop about ¼ of the batter onto the pan, spreading it out to a pancake about ½ inch thick.

3. Place 2 pieces of pork belly on top of the pancake, cover the skillet, and cook for 5 minutes.

4. Using a spatula, carefully flip the pancake over and cook, uncovered, for 4 minutes more.

FOR THE SAUCE

¼ cup Worcestershire sauce

¼ cup ketchup

2 tablespoons oyster sauce

1½ tablespoons sugar

TO MAKE THE SAUCE

1. While the pancake is cooking, make the sauce by mixing the Worcestershire sauce, ketchup, oyster sauce, and sugar together in a small bowl.

2. When the pancake is finished cooking on the second side, flip it over once more and brush some of the sauce over the top. Squeeze Japanese mayonnaise over the top (if using).

3. Serve hot, garnished with bonito flakes.

Ingredient Tip: Nagaimo and yamaimo are both Japanese yams with a high starch content, making them great binders. You can find fresh nagaimo/yamaimo in Japanese or Asian markets. Look for a long, hairy tuber with tan skin and white flesh. Since the juice can irritate the skin, you may want to wear gloves when grating it.

OCTOPUS DUMPLINGS (TAKOYAKI)

DAIRY-FREE, NUT-FREE

PREP TIME: 15 minutes / **COOK TIME:** 10 minutes

MAKES ABOUT 14 TAKOYAKI

Similar to okonomiyaki, this recipe uses a pancake-like batter to coat pieces of cooked octopus (*tako*), before they're cooked over high heat. To make Octopus Dumplings, you need a special mold that's usually nonstick or made of cast iron, similar to the pan used to make *ebelskiver* (Dutch pancake balls), so if you're unable to locate a proper takoyaki pan use an ebelskiver pan instead. The trick to making takoyaki is to flip the balls at just the right moment during cooking so that the batter is runny enough to run down into the bottom of the mold, making a spherical ball with the fillings in the center. A chopstick or bamboo skewer can be helpful.

FOR THE DUMPLINGS

1¼ cups Awase Dashi (page 25) or dashi made from store-bought powder

1 large egg

¾ cup all-purpose flour

¼ cup grated Japanese yam (nagaimo)

1 teaspoon baking powder

½ teaspoon kosher salt

Neutral-flavored vegetable oil, for greasing pan

3 ounces cooked octopus, cut into ½-inch pieces

¼ cup of finely sliced scallions, green and white parts

¼ cup tenkasu (tempura scraps, optional, page 191)

3 tablespoons Red Pickled Ginger (page 58)

TO MAKE THE DUMPLINGS

1. In a medium bowl, whisk together the Awase Dashi and egg.

2. In a large bowl, whisk together the flour, Japanese yam, baking powder, and salt. Whisk in half of the dashi mixture until it is well combined. Add the remaining dashi mixture and whisk to combine.

3. Set the takoyaki pan over medium-high heat and brush the wells with vegetable oil.

4. When the pan begins to smoke, pour the batter into the wells, filling them halfway. Add the octopus (about 2 pieces for each well), scallions, tenkasu (if using), and pickled ginger.

5. Pour additional batter on top, so that it fills up the wells and overflows just a bit.

6. Cook for 1 to 2 minutes, until the batter in the bottom of the wells has firmed up. Using a bamboo skewer or chopstick, flip the balls over, scraping away any excess batter. Continue to cook, flipping every 30 seconds or so, until the balls are cooked through and golden brown, about 4 minutes more.

FOR THE SAUCE

3 tablespoons Worcestershire
   sauce

1 teaspoon water or dashi

¾ teaspoon sugar

½ teaspoon ketchup

TO MAKE THE SAUCE

1. Make the sauce. In a small bowl, stir together the Worcestershire sauce, water, sugar, and ketchup.

2. Serve the dumplings hot, drizzled with the sauce.

Substitution Tip: *If you don't like octopus, substitute cooked shrimp or vegetables.*

PORK GYOZA

DAIRY-FREE, NUT-FREE

PREP TIME: 20 minutes / **COOK TIME:** 10 minutes

MAKES ABOUT 24 GYOZA

Gyoza are filled dumplings similar to Chinese pot stickers. These are filled with a seasoned pork and cabbage mixture, pan-fried until crisp on the bottom, then steamed until tender and cooked through. Serve them with ponzu dipping sauce, if desired.

8 ounces ground pork

1 cup shredded cabbage

1 (2-inch) piece fresh ginger, peeled and grated

1 garlic clove, grated

1 tablespoon soy sauce

2 teaspoons cornstarch

1 teaspoon sesame oil

1 scallion, thinly sliced

¼ teaspoon white pepper

Pinch kosher salt

1 (12-ounce) package gyoza wrappers

2 tablespoons neutral-flavored vegetable oil

½ cup water

1. In a medium bowl, combine the pork, cabbage, ginger, garlic, soy sauce, cornstarch, sesame oil, scallion, white pepper, and salt and mix well.

2. To make the gyoza, place one wrapper on your work surface and place about 1 teaspoon of the filling in the center. Wet your finger with water and use it to wet the edges of the wrapper, which will help with sealing. Fold the wrapper over the filling and seal. Pinch the edges to make little pleats along the seal. Repeat until all the filling has been used up.

3. In a large skillet, heat the vegetable oil over medium heat. Place the dumplings in the skillet in a single layer and cook until the bottoms turn brown and crisp, about 4 minutes. Add the water and immediately cover the skillet. Cook until the water has evaporated and the dumpling wrappers are tender, about 5 minutes more.

4. Serve hot.

Substitution Tip: *Make these gyoza vegan by omitting the pork and substituting an additional 2 cups of shredded cabbage and 8 ounces of chopped mushrooms. Stir-fry the cabbage and mushrooms with the other ingredients, for about 8 minutes, then let it cool before filling the wrappers.*

GLOSSARY

ASA-RA - the tradition of enjoying ramen for breakfast

ASSARI - a clear broth cooked for a shorter length of time

BENI SHOGA - red pickled ginger strips (pickled in plum vinegar)

BONITO - dried, smoked, and flaked tuna

CHASHU - sliced roasted pork

CHINTAN - a clear broth; also known as assari

DASHI - a seaweed-and-fish-based broth

DOUBANJIANG - a spicy bean paste

ITAMAE - head chefs

KAEDAMA - a second helping of noodles

KAMABOKO - a fish cake

KANSUI - an alkaline solution that creates the springy texture of ramen noodles

KIKURAGE - a wood ear mushroom

KOMBU - dried kelp

KOTTERI - an opaque broth made from long-simmering bones

MAYU - a black garlic oil

MENMA - fermented seasoned bamboo shoots

NARUTO - a type of kamaboko; a pink-and-white fish cake

NEGI - a Japanese long onion, also called Welsh onion

NIBOSHI - dried sardines and anchovies

NITAMAGO - a slow-cooked, soft-boiled egg

PAITAN - a white broth; also known as kotteri

RAMEN-YA - ramen shops

RAYU - a Japanese chili oil

SANSHO - a Sichuan numbing peppercorn

SEABURA - small chunks of pork fat

SHICHIMI TOGARASHI - a seven-spice mix condiment

TAKUAN - fermented daikon radish

TARE - seasoning sauce for ramen

TSUKEMEN - ramen noodles with the broth served separately for dipping

YATAI - mobile food stalls

REFERENCES

Orkin, Ivan. *Ivan Ramen: Love, Obsession, and Recipes from Tokyo's Most Unlikely Noodle Joint*. London: Bloomsbury Publishing Plc, 2014.

Shimbo, Hiroko. *The Japanese Kitchen: 250 Recipes in a Traditional Spirit*. Boston, MA: Harvard Common, 2012.

Tsuji, Shizuo, Mary Sutherland, M. F. K. Fisher, Ruth Reichl, and Yoshiki Tsuji. *Japanese Cooking: A Simple Art*. New York: Kodansha USA, 2011.

Yagihashi, Takashi, and Harris Salat. *Takashi's Noodles*. Berkeley, CA: Ten Speed Press, 2009.

...yes! Japan Ramen Magazine, ed. *Tokyo Ramen: Perfect Guide Book*. Tokyo, Japan: Suniwa Co, 2016.

MEASUREMENT CONVERSIONS

VOLUME EQUIVALENTS (LIQUID)

US Standard	US Standard (ounces)	Metric (approximate)
2 tablespoons	1 fl. oz.	30 mL
¼ cup	2 fl. oz.	60 mL
½ cup	4 fl. oz.	120 mL
1 cup	8 fl. oz.	240 mL
1½ cups	12 fl. oz.	355 mL
2 cups or 1 pint	16 fl. oz.	475 mL
4 cups or 1 quart	32 fl. oz.	1 L
1 gallon	128 fl. oz.	4 L

OVEN TEMPERATURES

Fahrenheit	Celsius (approximate)
250°F	120°C
300°F	150°C
325°F	165°C
350°F	180°C
375°F	190°C
400°F	200°C
425°F	220°C
450°F	230°C

VOLUME EQUIVALENTS (DRY)

US Standard	Metric (approximate)
⅛ teaspoon	0.5 mL
¼ teaspoon	1 mL
½ teaspoon	2 mL
¾ teaspoon	4 mL
1 teaspoon	5 mL
1 tablespoon	15 mL
¼ cup	59 mL
⅓ cup	79 mL
½ cup	118 mL
⅔ cup	156 mL
¾ cup	177 mL
1 cup	235 mL
2 cups or 1 pint	475 mL
3 cups	700 mL
4 cups or 1 quart	1 L

WEIGHT EQUIVALENTS

US Standard	Metric (approximate)
½ ounce	15 g
1 ounce	30 g
2 ounces	60 g
4 ounces	115 g
8 ounces	225 g
12 ounces	340 g
16 ounces or 1 pound	455 g

INDEX

ACKNOWLEDGMENTS

With love to my children, who are endless wells of inspiration and interruption. With gratitude to my father, who taught me to appreciate the beauty of food and books, to always order what the locals eat, and to make an incredible Japanese macaroni gratin. —NIY

I am forever grateful to my husband and son, who are always hungry for a bowl of ramen, no matter how many nights in a row I've served it for dinner, and to my parents for raising me to appreciate good food and teaching me to cook. —RD

We also want to express our great appreciation to Jesse Aylen, Kim Suarez, Wendy Simard, and the entire Rockridge team for their patience, expertise, and support in creating this ramen bible.

ABOUT THE AUTHORS

Naomi Imatome-Yun is a *Wall Street Journal*–bestselling author and editor-in-chief based in Los Angeles. She was a food editor and restaurant reviewer for more than a decade, built one of the most popular Asian food websites, and is the author of *Seoul Food Korean Cookbook* and other bestsellers. She loves demystifying the Japanese and Korean food she grew up making and eating.

Robin Donovan is a cookbook author, recipe developer, and blogger who is obsessed with Japanese food. She is the author of *Sushi at Home* and several other bestselling cookbooks, including *Campfire Cuisine: Gourmet Recipes for the Great Outdoors*. She lives in Berkeley, California, and blogs about easy, international recipes for people who love food at www.AllWaysDelicious.com.